#1 AMERICAN

PAUL ALLEN

BOB, JORD

I WOULD DO IT AGAIN

In the annals of war, no braver men have taken to the field of battle than the pilots who flew the iconic Huey helicopters during the Vietnam War. I saw their unwavering resolve time and again as they flew through withering gunfire to carry us safely away from the gates of eternity and bring us home. Bob Ford's account of his year in the command seat of his ship of salvation is a priceless contribution to the literary canon of that war.

—**David A. Maurer**
Special Forces Veteran
Author of *The Dying Place*

Serving as a crew chief in Hue was a life-changing experience. It was an opportunity to serve with the best of the best, the cream of the crop. The pilots and crews were fearless. The bonds grew so strong that today when we meet, we still feel the connection. The Hue experience and these dedicated men will always be in my heart.

—**Heidi (Bud) Atanian**
Crew Chief
Hue Detachment 282 Assault

When Lt. Ford joined the company, he rapidly became an aircraft commander. He soon commanded a detachment located in Hue, sixty-one miles from our company. During the Tet Offensive in January 1968, Bob and his crew flew hundreds of missions in support of US and ARVN troops. On all of these missions, they were under enemy fire. Bob exemplified the best qualities of an army aviator. He never let me down. I am proud of him.

—**Lt. Col. Chuck Ward, Retired**
Commanding Officer 282 Assault

I thought the book was exciting from start to finish. I feel I learned a lot about the Vietnam War and what the American soldiers, as well as the Australians and the South Vietnamese, went through. My favorite part in the first of the book was when Bob flew between two hills and got shot at. It was exciting, and I wanted to read more to find out what else would happen. The pictures were cool and helped me understand the story even more.

—**Alek Winter**
Age 12
Okeene, Oklahoma

-BLACK-
CAT 2-1

-BLACK-
CAT 2-1

The True Story of a Vietnam
Helicopter Pilot and His Crew

BOB FORD

BROWN BOOKS
PUBLISHING GROUP

Black Cat 2-1
The True Story of a Vietnam Helicopter Pilot and His Crew

Brown Books Publishing Group
16250 Knoll Trail Drive, Suite 205
Dallas, Texas 75248
www.BrownBooks.com
(972) 381-0009

A New Era in Publishing™

ISBN 978-1-61254-208-9 (HC)
ISBN 978-1-61254-896-8 (PB)
LCCN 2014952699

Printed in the United States
10 9 8 7 6 5 4 3 2

For more information or to contact the author, please go to
www.BlackCat2-1.com

To my kids, Amy, Allison, and Tyler, and their kids,
Emma, Cate, Tess, Nathan, and Taylor. You're the best,
and I'm proud of all of you. Also to Sherri and Geraldine
for their many hours of work helping me tell this story. And
to that dependable machine of flight, the UH-1 Huey.

In the Vietnam War, 2,197 helicopter pilots and 2,717 crewmembers were killed. This is the story of one pilot who made it home and the valiant men he served with who risked their lives for the troops on the ground.

Many good things came out of the Vietnam War. This memoir of personal experiences is one of them.

The Black Cats Hue detachment, NOV 67: standing, Lieutenant Bob Ford, W-2 Dwight Dedrick, W-1 Mark Skulborstad, and W-2 Tom Pullen; seated, W-1 John Aye, W-2 Al Toews, W-2 Jerry McKinsey, and W-1 Dick Messer

–Contents–

–Prologue–

0900, 11 NOV 90
Okeene, Oklahoma

I received a call from a local third grade teacher, Sandy Boeckman, who wanted me to speak to her class on Veterans Day. I had never spoken in public about Vietnam, and she could probably sense the hesitation in my voice, so she added, "Bob, these kids need to hear from a veteran." After that comment, there was no way I could refuse her.

I put on my green dress uniform. I hadn't worn it for twenty-four years, but it still fit. I also took along my flight helmet, a box of C-rations, dog tags, and some eight-by-ten photos that I put up on the chalkboard with magnets. I talked for about five minutes about the significance of Veterans Day and then asked for questions. The kids hesitated.

"There is no such thing as a dumb question in the army," I added. After that, all hands went up.

"OK, one at a time," I said. "I'll answer every question."

The first question was about a picture of the Huey helicopter I had flown in combat.

"How fast will it go?" the student asked, followed by, "Why is there a black cat on the front?"

About ten minutes later, a little girl stood up, pointed to the picture of me with seven other Hue detachment pilots, and quietly asked, "Did any of your friends get hurt?"

I looked at the photo and said, "Yes, sweetheart." My eyes rested on those faces I knew so well, and it was as if no time had passed.

Standing there in that third grade classroom, I was overcome with both grief and pride. I tried to answer her question three times but couldn't, and I froze as unexpected tears flowed down my cheek.

Sandy walked forward, handed me some tissues, and carefully answered the little girl's question for me. I pulled it together and did a good job the rest of the hour. The kids were courteous and attentive.

After the children left, Sandy approached me. "Bob, you must write your story," she told me. "You really should. People want to know."

So I did, and here it is.

−1−

GOING IN HOT

I'm in San Francisco, and I got processed in OK. Both arms are real sore from the eight shots they gave me. My stomach feels terrible from the malaria pill. I leave for Vietnam tonight at 2100 hours in a C141—no windows, seat backwards—for 18 hours. Met a lot of infantry lieutenants. All good guys. All of us admit we're scared. We had heard there was a one in seven chance of getting killed or wounded.

25 JUL 67 Letter to Diane

As our helicopter neared the landing zone, the radio barked, "Alley Cat 3-4, this is Black Cat 6." Alley Cat was the call sign for our gunships.

"6, this is 3-4, go."

"Roger, Alley Cat. Start your run at LZ tango."

"Roger, 6. Starting prep now. 3-4 out."

Hebert, the pilot, told the gunners we were going in hot, which meant our two door gunners were to shoot their M60 machine guns continually at any enemy or suspected enemy emplacement. Adrenaline rushed through me as I heard the explosions of the 2.75-inch rockets from the gunships finding their targets in and around the landing zone. I heard the sound of the M60s in the back of our ship start firing.

The landing zone (LZ) had been prepared by the gunships, and every ship in the lift had ample room to land. I did not see any enemy muzzle flashes. The troops jumped out and were gone within seconds. I was surprised when Hebert said, "You got it," which meant he was transferring control of the ship to me.

"I got it," I responded, taking control. Hebert lit a cigarette.

It was my fourth day in Vietnam.

★★★★

Light rain, the smell of human waste, and a mass of military activity—these had been my first impressions of the country. After a brief stop at Wake Island, we had landed at Pleiku, in the central highlands. I headed toward the Command Center to receive my first assignment. As I carried my army-issued air force duffel and L.L. Bean canvas bag, my legs felt like rubber from pure fear. Mud oozed through the airstrip's perforated steel planking.

After storing my gear, I was told there were no openings in the First Cavalry, so I spent the rest of the day familiarizing myself with the compound. I was given the location of a bunker in case of a rocket or mortar attack. The next morning, there was still no assignment. I was beginning to feel more relaxed. My fear of death was subsiding, but it was replaced by a fear of the unknown.

As I walked by a Quonset supply hut, I saw an infantry captain who looked like a real veteran. He wore regular olive drab fatigues and carried a pair of worn jungle fatigues that were faded from his year in the field. He started to toss the old fatigues into a small pile of discarded clothing near the hut, and I asked what he was going to do with them.

"Leave them right here," he answered.

He was about my size. I hesitated and then asked, "Do you think I could have them?"

He smiled slightly, sensing that I didn't want to look like a new guy, before giving them to me. "They're yours. They got me through this year."

Before he could walk away, I asked, "What does it take to make it through a year of flying helicopters?"

"Well, I'll tell you," he said. "You'll have to put personal safety aside and do everything you can for the troops on the ground. No matter what."

He spoke with such intensity that his words were permanently etched in my mind. I could tell he had respect for pilots and that he'd depended on them to stay alive. It made me proud to be an army aviator.

I had been in the country for two days, and I was still walking and breathing. The third day, I stood before the administrative officer, awaiting my assignment.

"Lieutenant Ford, you are to report to Major Meyers for assignment with the 17th Aviation Group in Nha Trang," he began. "They need lieutenants. If this weather subsides, we may be able to get you there today."

I liked the idea of being needed. This assignment meant I would get into the war. I felt calm and prepared, and within fifteen minutes, I was ready to be transported to my new destination. I boarded a noisy Caribou, a medium-size, twin-engine cargo airplane, and was on my way.

After landing in Nha Trang, I went in search of Major Meyers. A sergeant who ran the office with obvious efficiency greeted me, and then I reported as ordered and saluted the major. His desk was filled with papers, maps, and a nameplate that held a pen and pencil on each end. I chuckled to myself and thought, *This must be what the terms "desk jockey" and "paper-pusher" mean.*

On the wall behind Major Meyers's desk was a large map of South Vietnam divided among four corps. The northernmost was designated as I Corps. Within each area, the army aviation companies were labeled with their designated numbers. The 282nd was the farthest north within I Corps. As I looked at the map, I noticed red Xs next to each company and wondered what they meant. There were many more Xs next to the 282nd than any other company.

The major interrupted my thoughts. "Well, Lieutenant, I have just gone over your personnel file. Do you have any idea which unit you want to join? Do you have any friends stationed in country?" He walked toward the map.

"No, sir," I replied. "I'm the first guy in my flight class to get here."

"Take a look at the map, Lieutenant. Is there any location where you want to go?"

I looked at the red Xs at the top of the map near the 282nd. "Sir, what are those red Xs by each company?"

"Those, Lieutenant, are known aircraft hits from hostile fire in the past seven days."

"Do they need lieutenants, sir?"

"They always need lieutenants."

"That's where I want to go."

He looked at me. "Are you sure you want to go there?"

My gut feeling was that the year would pass more quickly if I were a part of the action, so I nodded. "Yes, sir, I'll go there."

The major assigned me to the 282nd Assault Helicopter Company stationed at Da Nang. He informed me that there would be a C-130 flight leaving the next morning at 7:00 a.m. Then he handed me my orders and added, "It will be interesting."

I was relieved as I left his office but still couldn't sleep that night due to the thought of getting into the cockpit the next morning and starting my tour. Unfortunately the C-130 heading to Da Nang was grounded due to rain so heavy that it was difficult to distinguish a building only fifty feet away. By the next morning, the rain had subsided, but the C-130 scheduled to transport me was once again grounded, this time due to a maintenance problem. Within an hour, however, things began to happen quickly.

I watched as a Huey approached a landing pad close to where I was waiting. On the front of its avionics cover was a large yellow full moon with a silhouette of a black cat with red eyes. It was impressive and exactly what I thought a combat insignia should look like.

The commanding officer (CO) of the 282nd, Major Chuck Ward, was flying the Huey and had come to Nha Trang just to pick me up. He returned my salute as he greeted me. He looked rock solid. I liked him immediately and sensed he felt the same toward me. He never shut the helicopter down as I climbed into the right seat.

Major Ward called the tower, "Black Cat 6 request clearance for takeoff." I liked the Black Cat call sign from the start.

I was surprised when Major Ward let me bring the Huey to a hover. We flew north along the coast at about two thousand feet above ground level to the Marble Mountain Air Facility located on the east side of Da Nang near the coast of the South China Sea. After three weeks without flying, it felt good to handle the controls.

As soon as we arrived at the 282nd Company headquarters, which was located on the southwestern side of the Marble Mountain active runway, I was told to fly copilot on an emergency combat assault. Combat-assault missions or CAs were one of our primary jobs. It was departing in fifteen minutes.

★★★★

I had only my flight helmet from flight school, which had just been painted olive drab. Since there had not been time to receive a bullet-proof chest protector or a sidearm, I asked, "Where do I get my gear?" But another pilot, who I assumed was an aircraft commander (AC), was already signaling me to climb aboard.

"Wait here," came a voice behind me. "I'll see what I can find."

Without saying another word, Specialist Fourth Class Baker was gone. As he walked briskly back toward me carrying an infantry-type flak vest, I could hear the Hueys going through their startup. Once he handed me the vest, I said thanks and started to run to the aircraft. He laughed as he said, "Relax, sir. They won't leave without us. I'm the crew chief on the ship you're flying." He pointed toward one aircraft and said, "That's mine. Climb in." I liked his calm, humorous attitude. It was the same Huey that the AC had been signaling me to board.

As we strapped into our seatbelts and harnesses, the door gunner pulled the pin holding the side of my armored seat and locked it into place. Because of the location of the locking pin, this procedure is almost impossible for a pilot to execute. I could hear the AC shout over the noise of the helicopter, which was already at flight idle, "Hey, Lieutenant, are you ready to go? Put your helmet on. Watch and listen."

As we proceeded to the LZ, he said over the intercom, "You never know about a new lieutenant." His voice was serious. "Now, if you listen to what all the aircraft commanders say, you'll be OK. Sometimes it's hard for a lieutenant to take orders from a warrant while in the aircraft. If you want to make it as a pilot and someday an aircraft commander, you had better get started now."

I was surprised by his bluntness but reasoned he must have had confrontations with new lieutenants in the past. He would get none from me. He was calm. He looked, acted, and flew like a real combat veteran in total control. He was typical of the aircraft commanders I was to meet. I wanted to be like them. This made the advice I received that day easy to follow.

As we flew fifteen hundred feet above the jungle, I was getting to know the crew by listening to their conversations over the intercom. The aircraft commander, W2 Harold Hebert (pronounced A-Bear), was considered an old combat veteran at the age of twenty-one. At 5'8" and about 130 pounds, he was lean and fit, and he had been in country for about nine months. I watched the instruments and took everything in as he perfectly maneuvered our ship in a seven-aircraft formation. I was getting my first taste of flying combat, and I loved it.

We were approaching the LZ when the radio burst to life. "Alley Cat 3-4, this is Black Cat 6."

"6, this is 3-4, go."

"Roger, Alley Cat. Start your run at LZ tango."

"Roger, 6. Starting prep now. 3-4 out."

Hebert told the gunners we were going in hot, and I heard the M60 machine guns in the back of our ship start firing. As we approached, I heard a series of explosions as the 2.75-inch rockets from the gunships found their targets in and around the LZ.

The LZ had been prepared by the gunships, so every ship had plenty of space to land. I watched for enemy muzzle flashes but saw none. The troops jumped out and were gone within seconds. I was surprised when Hebert said, "You got it," which meant he was transferring control of the ship to me.

There are two identical sets of controls for the aircraft, and there can't ever be confusion about who is flying. A pilot relinquishing control of the aircraft uses brief wording over the intercom such as, "You have the aircraft" or "You got it," which is followed by the second pilot's acknowledgment, "I have the aircraft" or "I got it." The transfer takes only a second or two. Then the pilot transferring the controls raises his hands to show he is off of his controls. "I got it," I said as I took control. Hebert lit a cigarette, and we were on our way back to pick up more troops.

Hebert let me fly the rest of the missions that day. We made two more insertions, and I felt myself improve each time. When we landed back at Marble Mountain, I felt proud and confident having passed my first test. I did not feel fear.

Nobody went out of the way to talk to me, which was typical treatment of a new guy. With the combat assault complete, I went in search of the supply sergeant. When I found him, he was chewing on the stub of a cigar, and I asked for the standard issue gear.

"Sir, before I can release any item, you are going to have to bring me requisition forms," he said and rattled off letters and numbers. "Then I may be able to help you."

I gave him a puzzled look while thinking, *What an odd request in a war zone.*

He erupted into laughter and said, "Lieutenant, I have to do this to each new guy. It breaks up the monotony. I'll get you what you need."

He gave me a .45-caliber Colt 1911 automatic pistol with a holster, jungle fatigues, two pairs of jungle boots, and bedding. I kept the flak vest since no chest protector was available. As I left, he said, "Good luck, sir. Keep your head down."

After storing my gear, I decided to check out the officers' club. Walking through the front door, I felt like I was in a World War I movie. The lighting was dim, and the place looked and smelled much as I would imagine a bar in a war zone. Inlaid on the floor by the door was a Halloween black cat arched in the middle of a full moon circle. It looked identical to the black cat on the front of our Huey. I stopped to look around. The one thing that caught my eye was a lone combat boot embedded in concrete at the end of the bar.

The first person I saw was my aircraft commander from the day's combat assault. Hebert sat at a table just past the inlay with three other pilots. I walked toward them, but the reception I received was not the one I expected. As I approached the table, a bell clanged. Hebert stood and said something about me doing pretty good today, but then he laughed and said, "Lieutenant, you are to buy a round for everyone in the bar."

I thought it was because I was a new guy. The other pilots started to laugh as Hebert continued, "You walked on the Black Cat, and anyone who steps on it owes a round to everyone in the club. It's a tradition."

As he spoke, I glanced around the room to see no less than ten officers. I did not like the idea of paying for their drinks because I never carried much money—I sent all my paycheck home with the exception of sixty bucks a month. But there was no way out of the predicament.

"If it's tradition, then I'm ready to pay up," I said. Beers were thirty-five cents, and mixed drinks were fifty.

Hebert explained that the boot belonged to our commanding officer, Major Ward, who had instructed it would be the duty of the newest company officer to keep the boot and the bell shining.

Buying a round for everyone wasn't so bad, but the thought of having to keep that boot polished, as well as the bell above the bar, ate at me. This was a war zone. I saw no sense in such silliness, but I kept my feelings to myself. I had no choice but to follow tradition, so I rounded up my Kiwi and Brasso polish and took care of them.

As I headed back to my sleeping quarters, which we called our "hootch," I saw three warrant officers who had been in the officers' club walking into a hootch. Hebert called for me to join them. As I walked in, Hebert said, "Hey, Lieutenant, I'd like to introduce you to Lennis Lee." A tall, thin man standing next to Hebert extended his hand and greeted me. He spoke with a down-to-earth North Carolina drawl.

Hebert continued, "This is Tom Woehl, the company standardization instructor pilot, or SIP. And here is the old man of the bunch. This is Easley."

At thirty-five, Gene Easley was old for a first-tour warrant. He was the only one in the room with the gunship platoon. Lanky and slow talking, I found him to be one of the most likable pilots in the company. He could play the guitar and sing quite well with his baritone voice, and he made up lyrics to familiar tunes.

The next day before I could start flying right seat as a copilot, or what we called the peter pilot, I was required to pass a check flight. The peter pilot nickname comes from the military flight logbook. There are two places to record flight time. The first is labeled "AC" for aircraft commander and the second "PP" for primary pilot or copilot. Even though I had already flown on a combat assault, it was standard operating procedure for any new pilot to complete and pass a check ride. My check ride came with Woehl, who put me through everything I had learned at Fort Wolters and Fort Rucker, as well as combat procedures. He was outstanding and as professional as any of the instructor pilots (IP) from flight school. He managed to make me feel comfortable, and the one-hour check ride went well.

I saw the crew chief who had rustled up the flak jacket for me to use on the previous day's combat assault. He told me about a detachment sixty-two miles north of Da Nang stationed at the old imperial capital city, Hue. I was impressed by what he told me about the reputation of the pilots and crews stationed there. I discovered they were highly regarded because so much was demanded of them. The crew chief said only three ships were responsible for serving the entire northern part of the I Corps. Their area of operation (AO) was from Hue to the Demilitarized Zone (DMZ) that separated North and South Vietnam and west to Laos. The detachment was comprised of eight pilots—four ACs and four peter pilots. From his description, I gathered these guys were in the air much more than those in Da Nang. They lived in a compound of about two hundred men and were removed from company and battalion officers, which was appealing to me.

I wanted to go to Hue, but when I next reported to Major Ward, he told me he needed me as a section leader with the second platoon. After Major Ward gave me the assignment, he asked, "Do you have any questions?"

I decided to ask if there was a section leader position at Hue.

"The lieutenant up there will DEROS in two months," he said. This meant Date Eligible Return from Overseas or going home. "I don't know if you will be ready by then. It takes at least five months to make aircraft commander, which is what you must be to command that detachment. We'll see."

"Sir," I said, "I would like to have a chance for it."

Major Ward looked right at me before he spoke. "Lieutenant, if you are that determined to try for it, I'll hold off assigning anyone to replace Lieutenant Morris."

Thanking him for the opportunity, I knew I had my work cut out for me. I wondered if I'd spoken prematurely but felt proud to make the commitment.

I began to focus on getting my combat act together. I studied maps and Signal Operation Instructions, called SOIs. These small, stapled-together sheets of paper contained codes for radio frequencies currently being used. SOIs changed every three to four weeks or any time they were suspected to have been compromised by the enemy.

I asked the experienced pilots how to pronounce the names of locations on the maps. I practiced proper combat radio procedures. A pilot must plan what he is going to say before keying the transmit trigger. It is a must in combat for an aircraft commander to be brief and correct.

Everything was going pretty well, but I still had the problem of that boot and bell. Polishing these things seemed like such a waste of time. It was embarrassing. Luckily, in ten days, a new officer came to the company and those two chores became permanent history to me.

I flew every chance I got. With Hebert's, Lee's, and Woehl's instructive leadership examples, I started my quest for AC orders with the hope of assuming the Hue detachment command. It was going to take a lot of flying to make aircraft commander in only six weeks.

−2−

EARNING MY WINGS

I'm not really scared because so much is depending on us. Have not seen the sun yet and probably won't 'til September. I bought a camera—Yashica 5000 from another pilot for $30—takes only slides.

30 JUL 67 Letter to Diane

Chuck Yeager, Sergeant York, Audie Murphy, Eddie Rickenbacker, Ike and Jimmy Doolittle—these are the men who first captured my imagination and instilled in me the feeling that every man should be willing to serve his country in the military. Now I had the opportunity to serve as an aircraft commander in Vietnam if I could prove my readiness in the next six weeks. I had a long way to go to be prepared, but I knew I had already overcome many obstacles just to make it this far.

★★★★

I was born August 4, 1944, in Shawnee, Oklahoma, about two and a half years after the Japanese bombing of Pearl Harbor that launched the United States into World War II. I had stern yet loving parents; an older brother, Bill; a beautiful older sister, Anne; and a younger sister, Peggy. I liked all of my teachers growing up and was blessed with a high school sweetheart, Pam McBee, and a no-nonsense basketball coach, Jerrell Chesney, all positive influences on my life.

13

I was frequently on my own from sunup to sundown with a slingshot, BB gun, or fishing pole in hand and came home just in time for dinner. I loved animals and once rescued and raised a litter of raccoons. Another time, I adopted a baby crow that roosted outside my bedroom window, which I taught to "attack" Peggy's ponytail and clearly say "Hello, Bob." I was wiry and quick and loved the outdoors, and I often thought that if I could go back in time, I'd want to be an Indian scout. I was always curious and constantly wanted to test my limits.

My father, Leslie A. Ford, was the president of Shawnee Milling Company, which my granddad, John Lloyd Ford, founded in 1906. I was proud of this heritage and spent my summers working at the mill. Following in my dad's and granddad's footsteps, I headed to the University of Oklahoma in the fall of 1962.

To help with managing the family business someday, I decided to major in business management and minor in marketing and finance. But another "minor" would send me on an unforgettable, life-altering adventure: the Reserve Officers' Training Corps (ROTC).

While President Kennedy was sending more military advisors to Vietnam, I was attending ROTC classes in the armory on campus at OU. President Kennedy believed the loss of Vietnam to communist rule would lead to the fall of the rest of Southeast Asia, but Vietnam was only a name on the map to me. I had no idea that within five years I would serve my country there. Yet by the end of my senior year, the Tonkin Gulf Resolution was a fact, and Vietnam was no longer strictly for the US Military Assistance Command, Vietnam (MACV).

My ROTC instructor, Captain Eldon Shroeder, had served in Vietnam as an infantry officer with the First Cavalry. I was curious from the start and asked him what would be the most rewarding experience—no matter how dangerous—and the best way to serve my country. I assumed he would say to be an infantry platoon leader, but much to my surprise, he responded with conviction, "Be a helicopter pilot!"

Since my military heroes were mostly fliers, I made up my mind right then. At the time, troops were sent overseas daily, and the conflict was called a "police action." I didn't see it that way. From what I had heard from my instructor, it was a war and one that we needed to win. I was faced with an important decision: I could attend graduate school or I could join either the army reserve or the national guard. Becoming a weekend warrior was not for me, so I chose immediate active duty. Since I wanted to become an army aviator, I was required to complete an extra year of flight school. This extra year classified me as an obligated volunteer for three years, or OBV-3.

In addition to two hours of college credit each semester, the ROTC required attending a summer boot camp where leadership skills were emphasized. I did this for six weeks at Fort Sill in Lawton, Oklahoma, between my junior and senior years at OU. I looked forward to all the challenges of boot camp, especially firing the M1 Garand rifle. I managed to make both KP—kitchen police—and guard duty fun.

Besides going to summer boot camp, the ROTC meant receiving forty dollars a month during my junior and senior years. This was much welcomed and needed date money. We were also issued a green Class-A uniform, which I wore to my graduation. In addition to the pride I felt, I saved the $5.25 required to rent a cap and gown. Out of approximately two thousand graduating students in the class of 1966, I was the only one in military uniform sitting in the north end of the football stadium.

When I received my diploma on June 5, 1966, I also received my commission as a transportation officer in the United States Army.

As with most things in the service, there is a tradition that goes along with receiving a commission. After my cute, quiet, always-smiling girlfriend, Diane, pinned gold second lieutenant bars on my shoulders, I was to hand a silver dollar to the first enlisted man who saluted me. It was the ROTC staff sergeant who stepped up, saluted, and said, "Congratulations, sir, *Lieutenant* Ford." As I returned his salute, he extended his hand palm up with a smile on his face.

I began active duty on July 16, 1966, attending the transportation officer basic course at Fort Eustis, near Newport News, Virginia. Whereas mottos from the other army divisions conjured images of bravery, such as the infantry's "Follow Me" and the artillery's "King of Battle," the transportation motto was simply "Spearhead of Logistics." Since we were typically transporting men and goods in trucks and jeeps, my buddies and I joked that the motto should have been "Beats Walking."

For me, it was just a layover before flight school, although there were some high points. Our weekends were filled with athletics and all-around fun, including one memorable night at the Fort Lee Officers' Club, a VIP-type installation just outside of Washington, DC. We watched as Jane Jayroe from Laverne, Oklahoma, was crowned Miss America. Earlier some high-ranking officers had asked me if Oklahoma had any girls pretty enough to be in this contest. Jane made me so proud of my home state that night, and I admire her to this day.

During the nine-week course, I was the first transportation officer to make a perfect score on the army physical fitness test in more than two years. The test was comprised of five events. I finished the forty-yard low crawl in twenty-two seconds; the horizontal ladder, completing seventy-nine rungs; a dodge, run, and jump course in twenty-one seconds; and a grenade throw scoring thirty-six out of forty. The final event was a mile run in fatigue pants and combat boots. A fellow officer from Yale advised me that if I stayed with him, I would beat the time of 6:14 needed to receive a perfect score. He had rowed crew at Yale and looked like a distance runner. We stayed together until the last 110 yards when he said, "Way to go. See you at the finish line." He took off and beat me easily by ten yards, but he had been right. By keeping up with him, I completed the mile in 5:54.

On two occasions during my time at Fort Eustis, I obtained some "stick time" in a Bell H-13 Sioux, a two-bladed, single-engine light helicopter, at a nearby army airfield. While I was allowed to handle the cyclic and pedals, I was permitted only to feel the collective. The collective, when pulled upward while rolling in more throttle to the engine, increases power to the main rotor blades. The cyclic controls the rotating plane of the main rotor blades. By moving the cyclic, a pilot controls the aircraft's direction in flight. The pedals control the tail rotor to counteract torque from the main rotor and change direction at a stationary hover. In a short time, I was able to handle the controls smoothly, and the experience made my soon-to-follow first attempts at flying easier.

By October 1966, I was stationed at Fort Wolters near Mineral Wells, Texas, home of the US Army Primary Helicopter School. New student pilots try to absorb their surroundings and every word spoken. All 105 officers in my class, 67-10, were looking forward to their first flight with our instructor. There were two informative posters by the preflight briefing room door that opened to the tarmac where the helicopters were parked on the flight line. One warned to bend over when approaching or exiting a Hiller OH-23-D Raven on the ground when the rotor blades were spinning. It read, "The OH-23-D main rotor can flex down to four feet. How tall are you?" The other poster stated, "You will <u>not run</u> on the tarmac. However, there is no speed limit on walking."

I received my first real experience in a cockpit as I handled the controls of an OH-23-D. My stocky Southwest Airways civilian IP, J. L. Walker, monitored my every move. Like most of the students, I overcorrected the aircraft while on the practice field. After a couple of hours though, I improved and felt it would only be a short time before I soloed.

After a few more flights with the IP, I felt I had a knack for flying. Handling the emergency techniques such as autorotation, which is landing the helicopter without engine power to the rotor blades, took more time.

A day before my first solo flight, my IP pulled me to the side and said, "OK, Ford. If I had my way, you'd have your solo wings even though you don't have the required seven hours. But you will be the first one in this class to receive them."

The next day, we were about to leave the Da Nang Stage Field about seven miles north of the main heliport in Mineral Wells. I had just completed a practice autorotation without any assistance from my IP. As the helicopter skids touched the ground, he looked at me and said, "I'm going to walk over there and wait. Take it up and fly three traffic patterns."

As soon as he was clear of the main rotor and gave me a thumbs-up, I lifted the helicopter off the ground and flew the traffic patterns. The flight lasted about fifteen minutes. When I was back on the ground, my IP got into the aircraft and said, "Congratulations, Ford. How did you like it?"

With a feeling of accomplishment, I answered with a grin that it felt good to be the only one in the cockpit. I started to add "and much lighter" but didn't.

"You're one of the best I've had," he continued. As I accepted his praise, he stopped abruptly, pointed his finger within six inches of my nose, and said, "Now don't get cocky!" His advice has stayed with me.

After completing my first solo flight, my classmates carried out a military tradition by throwing me into the closest water available. It was a half-full drainage ditch they found during the bus ride back to the main heliport. Since it was November, the cold water chilled me to the bone. The rest of my classmates were thrown into the nice clean hotel pool at the Mineral Wells Holiday Inn after their solos.

I was pleased to be the first in my class to solo. After debriefing at the operations building back at the main heliport, I hurried to take my yellow cap, which was used to identify my flight class, to a seamstress to have my solo wings turned right side up.

Several weeks later, I was one of three officers chosen for an experiment. We were taken out of our officer flight-training course to train with the warrant officer candidates (WOCs) in the Hughes TH-55 Osage, which we nicknamed the "Mattel Messerschmidt." The WOCs were enlisted men who after passing a battery of tests were admitted to flight school. They wanted to fly more than anything else. After graduation, they would become a single-specialty type officer—warrant officer army aviator. I found my training with them both challenging and rewarding.

Transitioning to another helicopter after only two months of student training was not easy. All of the flight characteristics of the TH-55, especially emergency procedures, were quite different from the Hiller H-23. They even looked different. The experiment tested whether we could catch up and complete the next two months of full training. I soloed after two hours and caught up with the training requirement. The other two lieutenants with me in the experiment had difficulty. To my knowledge, the transition to another aircraft this early in training was never attempted again with student pilots.

For me, the reward came from the relationships I built with the WOCs. Even as a twenty-two-year-old, I thought these pilots looked young. I respected them for their seriousness, eagerness to learn, patriotism, and terrific attitudes. I had a strong gut feeling that when I flew in combat, these were the type of guys I wanted with me. Their humor and enthusiasm was contagious. Looking back, this second phase of flight school, which took place during the third and fourth months of my training, was the most enjoyable. Not only did I like getting to know the WOCs but also I had the most fun flying. Soloing in confined areas, landing on pinnacles, and going on cross-country flights day and night made me feel as if I were experiencing flying at its best.

In addition to flight school, I had something else on my mind. My girlfriend, Diane, had agreed to become my bride, and I couldn't have been happier. During the five months of training at Fort Wolters, we planned our wedding. Many parties were thrown in our honor, but my training schedule permitted me to attend only two. We scheduled the big day for the end of February because I would be close to completing my training.

On Friday, February 24, 1967, I drove to Oklahoma City for a Saturday afternoon wedding in a church overflowing with family and friends, and afterward, at the Oklahoma City Golf and Country Club, Al Good and his orchestra played swing-era classics at our reception into the night. Everything was perfect—except there would be no time for a honeymoon. I was scheduled to be back on the flight line at Fort Wolters by five o'clock on Monday morning.

We spent our wedding night at the nearby Howard Johnson's bridal suite and drove to Mineral Wells the next day. Early Monday morning, I arrived at the flight operation room at Dempsey Airfield before 5:00 a.m. While the operations officer briefed us on weather and aircraft assignments, my mind was elsewhere. I didn't hear a word. Next my IP, a captain, told us his expectations for the day's training flight. Toward the end of his briefing, he suddenly stopped, stood up, and got everyone's attention by yelling, "All right, listen up!" He waited until everyone was looking directly at him and slowly said, "How many in here want to be in the same sky with Lieutenant Ford today?"

Each pilot yelled in unison, "No, sir!"

Apparently everyone had been advised of my weekend's activities. The IP chuckled and said, "Lieutenant, you just flew an hour and fifteen minutes." As he wrote the hours into my flight log, he instructed me to go back to the motel and not to be late for the afternoon ground school. He didn't have to tell me twice. I made the one and a half miles back to the motel in record time.

Within two weeks, Diane and I departed for advanced training at Fort Rucker, Alabama. I had set high expectations for myself, and the next two months of intense instrument flight training did not come easily. The daily time spent in the Link trainer, a hydraulic mechanical trainer that simulated flight conditions, was tedious and demanding. The Link trainer was developed to train pilots to fly "blind" using only instruments as guides, which was much more difficult than what I had done to date. I couldn't get by any longer just flying by the seat of my pants. Instead I was required to do things methodically by the numbers.

I found myself back in the cockpit of a Bell H-13. This time, however, the cockpit was blacked out in strategic places so that our vision was restricted to only the instruments. For two months, we never saw the ground or the horizon while flying. On one occasion, I attempted to lean my head back to peek through the restricted vision components of my flight helmet. My IP was quick to admonish me and threatened to give me a pink slip, which was the equivalent of an unsatisfactory ride. I never tried it again. It took the entire course before I felt comfortable flying by instruments, but the training proved to be invaluable and would later save my life a few times in Vietnam.

The final two months of training took place in the Bell UH-1 Iroquois, which was called the Huey. It was the aircraft I would fly in Vietnam. I felt confident in the cockpit. It is a wonderful, powerful, smooth aircraft, and I couldn't wait to fly it in action. It was like strapping yourself to a Corvette that could fly. But just twenty-one days before graduation, I was called to the student headquarters for a telephone call from a captain stationed at the Pentagon.

"Lieutenant, you have been selected to report to Fort Eustis for AMOC training," he said.

I could hardly believe what I heard. The mere idea of attending Aircraft Maintenance Officer Course training almost made me sick to my stomach. A wave of thoughts flooded through my head: *Maintenance? Be in charge of a maintenance hangar? Become a mechanic?* I asked the captain to repeat his words and was just as shocked. I took a deep breath and calmly told him, "No, thank you, sir." As forcefully as I could muster, I stated, "That is not for me, sir."

The conversation was over. Two days later, another call came. This time, a major delivered the same request and persuasion. As before, I declined. During the next two weeks, I received two more telephone calls requesting that I attend AMOC, and each time the officer on the other end had been upgraded.

With only seven days left before graduation, I received one more call. This time the caller identified himself as a brigadier general. Setting formalities aside, he barked, "Lieutenant, you will report to Fort Eustis, Virginia! You will take AMOC training!"

"Well, sir," I responded, "how about if I do my tour in Vietnam and then decide about AMOC?"

The general fell silent for some time. I imagine he was trying to decide whether he could persuade me to accept the assignment. By now, I was aware that I could not be ordered to AMOC because it would have required my accepting an additional year past my three-year commitment.

For two minutes, which felt more like ten, the general bombarded me with questions and tried his best to convince me that maintenance was where I should be. Although my uniform was becoming saturated with sweat, I knew that if I could just keep him talking, I would eventually win. As he continued, I envisioned having to explain to my friends and brother that I was going to be a mechanic after telling them that I was going to fly in combat.

Finally the general got so agitated at my determined sidestepping that he asked in a voice as cold as ice, "Well, Lieutenant, just what do you want to do?"

I told him with a raised voice, "Sir, I want to go to Vietnam, serve my country, and fly in combat."

"Then, Lieutenant, that's just what you're going to do!" The next thing I heard was the receiver slam down. I had finally won.

Two days later, I received my orders for Vietnam. I would be the first in my class to go, arriving just twenty-one days after graduation.

A week before I was to leave, Continental United States orders came in the mail promoting me to first lieutenant. That had a nice ring to it. No more gold bars, which we called "butter bars." The single silver bar made me look as though I had been in the army for some time. Combined with silver aviator wings, they made my plain khaki uniform look quite snappy.

Diane and my brother, Bill, saw me off from the Will Rogers World Airport in Oklahoma City. Bill was two years older than I, athletic, and an Eagle Scout. Like my dad, he set an outstanding example of character. He had completed two years of active duty as an Army Artillery Officer and had just earned his master's degree in business at OU.

Not much was said in the final moments before I boarded the plane. Both of them knew I was ready to go. Still, our hearts were filled with anxiousness and fear.

The commercial aircraft took me to San Francisco where I received numerous immunizations, including cholera, smallpox, typhoid, tetanus, and typhus. Later in Vietnam, I would get two plague vaccinations.

The next morning, I boarded a C-141 Starlifter. The aircraft was Air Mobility Command's first jet aircraft designed to transport troops and cargo. We all sat backward on canvas jump seats.

With no windows to look out during the eighteen-hour flight, I had time to think about where I was headed and what I would face. As we crossed the Pacific Ocean, the fear of death was on my mind, and I wondered whether I would ever see my family again.

—3—

GAINING EXPERIENCE

The war came more into reality yesterday. Our gun platoon, the Alley Cats, had a bad day.

===================== 13 AUG 67 Letter to Diane

I had been in country three weeks and flew whenever possible. I constantly thought about becoming an aircraft commander and taking over the Hue detachment. The ACs in the second platoon never hesitated to let me fly, and when I told them how much I appreciated this, they told me I had earned it. I grew more confident every day.

It was evident that Lee, Woehl, and Hebert trusted me. Lee let me fly from the left seat on a few missions, and the difference at first was challenging. Everything felt out of place. I had wanted to try the left seat, and I didn't have to ask to do so before Lee suggested it.

Combat-assault missions usually involved seven to ten helicopters taking infantry into an area to be a blocking force or a moving force. For the latter, we inserted the troops close to the enemy to force them in the direction of a waiting ambush. Whatever the mission, there were always surprises. A lot of planning was involved, which took place the night before the CA. The terrain, the size of LZs, where to pick up the infantry, the weather, the radio frequency to be used, and how many troops were to be inserted were a few of the important components to consider.

On one of my first combat assaults, there were more aircraft than aircraft commanders available to fly. The company officers, including

Major Ward, decided to have me fly with another copilot, W1 Colburn. He looked like a laid-back California surfer, with a personality to match. He had been in country three months longer than I had, but I had more time in the left seat. Since neither of us had our AC orders, we both logged pilot time. Colburn and I decided that I would be the acting AC. There would be nine aircraft in our formation that day. The intelligence briefing indicated there would be several small single-ship LZs and marginal weather. Our commanders must have had confidence in us. There had never been a mission flown in the 282nd by two peter pilots in the cockpit.

We were flying number three or four in trail formation. As I approached the landing area on a short final, another helicopter cut us off in the last few seconds from our selected LZ. All of the LZs were spread out on the side of a sloping mountain. The aircraft that cut in front of my flight path decelerated, so I abruptly pulled back on the cyclic and quickly compensated to avoid a mid-air collision. Then, suddenly, we lost all air speed.

When I attempted to go to an alternative LZ, I experienced what's called "settling" with power. That happens when the aircraft is so heavy—as we were with a full load of combat troops—that it cannot hover unless you get a ground effect to help push air back up through the rotor blades. I pulled in more power to stop my descent, which slowed the rotors until the low revolutions per minute (RPM) audio warning sounded in our flight helmets. The warning, a shrill *woop*, *woop*, *woop*, is a bad sound for any helicopter pilot. We were in real trouble. I had to do something, and it had to be right because we were about five seconds from crashing into the side of the mountain.

I glanced left to see if we were clear and put pressure on the controls to go that way. At that instant, Colburn said over the intercom,

"Go right!" I knew I could trust him. I dove right and pushed on the right tail rotor pedal to assist the diving turn without looking. In a few seconds, the rotor RPM sped up and airspeed returned nicely. I made a go-around and landed the troops.

Colburn knew from experience that by going right with the torque of the rotor, we would gain RPM much faster. If I had gone left, further settling would have occurred and probable disaster. We went back to the pick-up zone, loaded more troops, and made two more insertions.

After three additional insertions, the CA was complete, and we headed home. We were flying behind the lead aircraft at five hundred feet above ground level due to deteriorating weather. I asked the lead aircraft to put his navigation lights on bright steady. Even though we were fairly close with about fifty feet between us, we lost him in a cloud. I instantly broke to the right and away from the lead aircraft. We flew down to the deck to avoid anyone behind us. I flew the aircraft low level, at one hundred knots toward the coast. Colburn decided on a heading of approximately 050 degrees to minimize our time over enemy territory. It took ten long minutes before we broke over the coast—a welcome sight.

We stayed four hundred meters off shore to keep us out of effective range of enemy small arms and flew a heading of 320 degrees, following the coast back to Marble Mountain. When our low fuel warning light came on, we knew we had twenty minutes of fuel left on board. Colburn pushed the start button of the minute sweep hand on the clock. This let us know how much time in minutes we had left before our fuel was exhausted. We calculated we could get home, and we did, within ten minutes of running out of fuel. We were relieved to be back at company headquarters, but the experience was invaluable. Pilots never want to run out of either air speed, altitude, luck, or experience. We almost ran out of all four at the same time. I'm glad we lived through it.

Colburn and I flew together on two more CAs a week later. Six months and seven hundred combat missions later, Colburn would be in the cockpit with me again during my most challenging month of flying, February 1968.

Three days after our close call, I had a 5:00 a.m. takeoff for another CA. That day, Hebert and I flew together. After all the South Vietnamese troops were on the ground, we stayed and flew all day to support the ground operation. We had taken gunfire but no hits to the aircraft. Unlike Lee, Hebert always flew left seat. He did let me fly most of the missions, which included resupply for the troops into the night.

After we returned to headquarters at Marble Mountain and shut down, Hebert turned on the overhead map lights, which had a red lens to protect night vision. He looked directly at me and said, "Ford, look at these eyes." He had my attention. Hebert pointed to the corner of his right eye, squinted, and said, "You're going to have eyes that look like this before you leave here."

In the dim red light, I couldn't tell at first if he was kidding me or not. A moment later, I could tell he was dead serious. He thought he had become much older, and his eyes reflected it. I said, "Oh, uh, really?"

"You sure will. Go ahead and fill out the logbook." Hebert had told me when we first met that it felt like he had been in Vietnam all his life. His life before going to Vietnam seemed too distant to remember much.

When he left the cockpit, I unbuckled my harness, relaxed, and loosened my newly acquired chest protector. The heavy vest plate was made of porcelain and steel and covered my entire chest. It weighed about twenty pounds. We nicknamed them our "chicken plates." I started to fill out the logbook, which took some time. We needed to record accurately all the flight times, landings, troops carried, amount of supplies, and, of course, any maintenance concerns. I had finished and returned the logbook to the designated slot behind the middle console when something struck me. I retrieved the logbook, opened it, and apparently spoke out loud. "Well, my gosh. Today's my birthday."

I hadn't realized that day was August 4. The door gunner walked by carrying two M60 machine guns and said in a barely audible voice, without looking my way, "Happy birthday, Lieutenant."

That was my twenty-third birthday, and I couldn't help but wonder if I would see twenty-four.

A week later, I was flying with Hebert on a typical mission south of Da Nang. We called it the Hoi An Run. We would radio the MACV HQ at Hoi An and give them our ETA. After landing at Hoi An, we loaded up and took everything from C-rations and new SOIs to ammunition and American advisors to different outposts, one of which was Tam Ky. Hebert let me fly the entire time. Everything was going smoothly—takeoffs, landings, and radio communications. We were flying at about fifteen hundred feet above ground level when Hebert performed his cigarette trick.

He put a cigarette on his flattened left hand between his two middle fingers with the filter end just over his fingertips. He then slapped the palm with his right hand, and the cigarette jumped toward his mouth. He caught the filter end neatly with his lips and ended the trick by popping his Zippo lighter open with one hand while the other snapped the wheel to ignite the flame. I never saw him miss.

Everything was starting to feel comfortable. I was able to come from altitude much faster and land more smoothly. I performed these procedures every time it was possible, including my landing at Tam Ky. While unloading supplies, one of the senior advisors within the compound told us we were taking a lot of small-arms fire on our approach. Our door gunners reported negative gunfire, and both of us in the cockpit confirmed. The senior advisor now insisted the fire was from a location where there had been suspected enemy activity. The location was about one kilometer or klick from the LZ.

Two of our gunships, B Model Hueys, were in the area and, as usual, were monitoring our radio transmissions. They came our direction and were close within minutes. Warrant Officer Easley was the AC in the lead ship.

The terrain around Tam Ky is mostly rice paddies with a few tree lines and small villages—not a lot of places where an enemy concentration could locate. As we were going back toward Hoi An, we told Easley the location of the suspected fire. He said he would confirm.

Within twenty-five minutes, we were back from Hoi An with our second run to Tam Ky and were told that the fire we received was from a concentration of the North Vietnamese Army. Easley and the other Alley Cat were ready to escort us in. By his voice, we could tell he was looking forward to expending his ordnance on the suspected enemy location. The Alley Cats carried a variety of weapons, including 2.75-inch rockets, mini guns, and the thumper—an automatic 40-millimeter grenade launcher. They also had two door gunners who shot M60 machine guns suspended from bungee cords.

Easley came in higher and behind us as we approached the LZ. He quickly closed in, passing in a forty-five-degree dive, and started firing. This was great to watch. The gunships covered the suspected area with precision. They then broke off to prepare for another run. These guys were good, and I felt safe with them as our escort. If there were enemies on the ground, they were in real trouble.

We unloaded the aircraft in no great hurry. Easley transmitted to our ship, "We covered the area. Think we'll make another run and check for any activity."

We became airborne and made a climbing left turn away from the target area in time to watch the Alley Cats make another run. This time, instead of breaking off at altitude, they continued over the target area at about two hundred to three hundred feet. Easley's lead gunship suddenly made an abrupt, erratic move left, then right. The radio was silent, so Hebert transmitted, "Alley Cat 3-8, this is 2-9."

In an excited near-scream, we heard, "Black Cat, Easley has been hit! Real bad!"

I felt my gut constrict. The copilot in Easley's ship recovered his composure and said almost calmly that he was proceeding to the Chu Lai medevac pad. He was experienced enough to know it was the closest and best place to go.

After a few radio transmissions from the Alley Cats and from our ship back to company HQ, we were told to go pick up Major Ward and take him to Chu Lai. We took twenty minutes to arrive at Marble Mountain, and then we refueled hot and proceeded to Chu Lai with Major Ward.

The first thing we saw there was Easley's B-model off to the side. We landed beside it, shut down, and talked to the crew. They were stunned. They were glad to see Major Ward, who had a fatherly effect on all the troops.

We walked into the hospital, which consisted of a series of long one-story wooden structures connected by narrow wooden walkways. The smell of purifying agents was strong. Major Ward immediately found a corpsman to ask where Easley was located. Hebert and I followed our CO in silence. As we entered another typical building, a doctor stood in our way. He recognized us as aviators and asked, "Any of you Hebert?"

Major Ward identified Hebert and told the doc he was Easley's CO. "How's Easley?" the major asked.

"Not good," the doc said. "We recovered the bullet. He's paralyzed. He was hit in the neck by a .30-caliber carbine."

I was surprised a doctor would know what kind of bullet it was. He was right. He handed us the .30-caliber round that looked perfect except for the grooves from the rifling and a small nick close to the nose.

We entered the room and saw Easley at a distance in a portable iron lung. I felt like I shouldn't be there. I was a new guy, but there I was witnessing everything. I didn't say a word. Major Ward and Hebert talked softly to Easley, who responded in a labored voice.

I only remember him saying, "Herby, the war is over for me. Tell my wife I love her."

I looked at Easley and wondered if that was going to be me someday.

"You'll pull through, Gene," Hebert said. "Don't worry."

I grew light-headed as I watched Easley struggle for words, and I found myself thinking, *Don't pass out. Not here in front of everyone.* Only a few weeks in country and I was watching this guy die before my eyes.

Major Ward or Hebert said something to the effect of, "We're leaving now. We'll see you back in Da Nang in a few months." Then we left his room.

Recently Major Ward wrote me about what he remembered of our brief encounter with Easley: "When I went to see Gene Easley within an hour of his being shot, he told me that he asked the doctor if he would ever again be able to play the piano. The doc said, 'Sure, son—better than ever!' Easley said, 'Boy, that is great—I never could play the darn thing before.' As you remember, Gene was an accomplished musician—just not a pianist."

That day after our visit with Easley, Hebert told me more about the dying pilot, almost showing his emotional side. Easley had already been in country a while, and the two had become good friends.

About three days later, we had just flown in from a mission when Woehl met us at the ship and said, "I'm sorry, but Gene Easley died this morning."

My body flinched and felt flush. I knew Hebert felt worse about it than I did, but he showed no emotion. As I observed Herbert handling the situation, I had the feeling I was evolving emotionally and rapidly adapting to death in combat. I was emulating Hebert's non-emotional response. Even though I felt badly for Easley, I was thankful it did not happen to me. After writing a letter home, I thought only about how to improve as a pilot and the missions to be flown the next day. I slept well.

Many years later, I got a call from Easley's wife. I recounted the words I heard from her husband and could tell it gave her a peaceful feeling to hear that she was on his mind. I assured her again that she definitely was. I told her how after that day, that experience, I promised myself I would get tougher and never let my guard down. She was gracious and said it gave her comfort to know that something good came of that incident, that maybe it got me home.

—4—

MARINE RECON

0400 preflight; 0445 chow; 0530 Special Forces pickup; flew with them till noon southwest of Da Nang; CA 1300 till 1900; 2100 lightning bug till 0200 . . . full day.

22 AUG 67 Letter to Diane

I experienced my first rocket attack during the third week of August. They came in at 2:00 a.m. without any warning. The screaming roar from the rockets' propellant was deafening, and all my senses froze as I tried to figure out what was happening. When the rockets came over our hootches on their way to our helicopters 150 meters north of our living quarters, they were no higher than one hundred feet above us.

The three five-and-a-half-foot rockets were Russian made and packed a tremendous wallop. Their inbound trajectory was somewhat flat and originated two to three miles southwest of our facility. I had observed an Honest John rocket firing at Fort Sill during ROTC summer boot camp, and nothing had compared to that noise until this. These inbound rockets were closer and much louder and had an impressive explosive impact. Nothing survived a rocket hit at its impact point.

One Huey was destroyed. The helicopters were in individual revetments, which were U-shaped protective structures constructed of sand-filled, fifty-five-gallon barrels, two on the ground and one on top. The other rockets landed harmlessly on the tarmac one hundred meters from the aircraft. Each rocket blew a hole about eight feet in diameter and three feet deep.

During the week of the rocket attack, I first encountered some of the men stationed at Hue. The crew chiefs, who had volunteered to go to Hue, stayed there as long as their ships did not need a periodic inspection or have serious maintenance problems. The ship's crew chief and the maintenance team in Da Nang completed periodic inspections every one hundred flight hours, which could take two days. Intermediate inspections were routine and could be performed every twenty-five hours.

The door gunners at Hue were all second-tour infantrymen who had requested assignment at Hue knowing they would get to engage the enemy with their M60 machine guns almost every day.

I encountered the Hue pilots on the flight line in Da Nang before a CA. I was impressed. These guys stood out from the rest of the company pilots. Their jungle fatigues were clean but by no means pressed. They never greeted anyone, nor did they report to platoon or company officers. Unlike any of us stationed at Da Nang, the Hue pilots were issued M16s and always carried them when exiting their aircraft. They looked combat ready. I heard then, and to this day I have not been told differently, that the Hue pilots who lived in the MACV Compound were the only pilots in Vietnam who manned the perimeter in case of enemy attack.

Carrying their issued M16s made them look a combat step above other pilots. I got the feeling they saw the war more closely and more often than everyone else. They had an independent assuredness. As much as I wanted to, I did not approach them. They showed no interest in talking to me, a new lieutenant. I wondered if I could fit in with that bunch, and I would find out in three weeks.

I flew as much as possible whenever missions were assigned in the Hue area of operation. I was getting to know the AO as well as any pilot stationed at Da Nang. Lee always let me fly half the time in the left seat, though Hebert and Woehl never did. Lee and Hebert introduced me to low-level flying, which was within three feet of the ground. Both emphasized the importance of flying low level into any location along the DMZ. You had to low level in and out of these outposts and firebases to keep from attracting artillery from the North Vietnamese Army. Also, just as importantly, you needed to be able to navigate in case bad weather forced you to the deck to complete your mission.

Flying more than one hundred knots—about 116 miles per hour—three feet off the ground means you really have to have your skills working at 100 percent. You must stay one instant ahead of any possible problem or obstacle because everything happens much more quickly. You don't consciously move the controls but literally think ahead of the aircraft and know what it will do before it does it.

Subconscious movements of the controls are more like applying pressure. The cyclic stick hardly moves more than the radius of a quarter. I got faster and more confident, and soon I began to look forward to low-level flying. When I glanced down at my tail rotor pedals through the clear Plexiglas, the Earth was a blur passing under my ship.

On August 22, 1967, I flew one of my longest days, which I recorded in a letter home.

> *0400 preflight inspection of the aircraft.* Each pilot visually inspected every component for movement or play of every nut and bolt, safety wire, coupling, and so on. It easily took fifteen minutes of close inspection and observation. I liked

to do my preflight inspection with the crew chief. The crew chiefs were better than I was at this, and I always complimented their professionalism.

0455 chow. Chow at the mess hall was good—chipped beef gravy on toast, which we called SOS, powdered scrambled eggs, recombined milk (powdered milk and water), and sometimes pancakes.

0530. Special forces contacted us and we flew supplies into the jungle outposts until noon southwest of Da Nang.

1300 until 1900. We married up with the company and participated in a combat assault.

2100 until 0200. I volunteered for a lightning bug mission, sometimes called a firefly, where a Huey flew about one thousand feet above ground level with two gunships overhead. The Huey shone an intense searchlight from the cargo section on any suspected enemy locations to look for movement or targets. An extra man was on board to handle the searchlight. We tried to draw gunfire, and when we did, the light would go out and the door gunners returned fire. Simultaneously the gunships unloaded their weapons on the enemy.

It was a long day with twelve hours of recorded flight time. I never really got too tired because I was on full alert until we shut down after the last mission. Only then did fatigue set in. I filled out the logbook during the required two minutes of engine cooldown at flight idle. After engine shutoff, I put my flight helmet on the small metal hook above my head, unbuckled my harness, and loosened my chest protector. I felt as if I could have fallen asleep right there in the cockpit.

A couple of days later, Lee and I were assigned to go north into the Hue area of operation. It was September 5, and we were diverted on an unusual mission to fly support for the marines. I'm not sure if the marine helicopters were grounded. It was the first time we flew in direct support.

Flying with Lee was always a good experience because his calm demeanor reflected trust, and I could fly more aggressively. He was instructional but never critical in that laid-back North Carolina accent of his. He had received his AC orders seven months earlier. I flew my best with him.

We reported to the marines on the east side of Marble Mountain's active runway, which was shared between the US Army and Marines. We were loading supplies to take to some of their troops into the field when a major approached us with noticeable concern. He said, "OK, men, unload the supplies. We have a recon team that needs extracting now! They have been out in the bush for eight days and are low on all supplies. The last two days, they have made enemy contact and are being chased."

A forward air controller that flew a small single-engine airplane had picked up their radio transmission. Their batteries were weak but strong enough for us to get coordinates. We conferred and marked the location of the recon team on our map.

"These guys are really hurting," the major said. "Try to get close to pick up their radio signal. Hopefully they still have smoke grenades. They need extraction."

The major was matter of fact, but the gravity of the situation was obvious to all of us. We needed to find them and get them out now.

The coordinates indicated forty klicks, about twenty-five miles, southwest of Da Nang. The few supplies on board were quickly off-loaded. Lee was visibly ready to get started. Taking care of troops in trouble always motivated us. It didn't matter at the time what the enemy conditions were; we just knew we were going to help some marines. We were given a frequency on the FM radio to contact the recon team, and we headed toward the mountainous jungle, briefing the crew chief and gunner over the intercom about the situation.

As we reached the location on the map, Lee transmitted on the FM frequency. "Kilo foxtrot, this is Black Cat 2-2." This was Lee's call sign. Numbers over the radio are always spoken in single digits, so twenty-two is said "two-two." "Niner" is used instead of nine because nine and five sound identical when transmitted over the radio.

Lee pressed the microphone trigger switch on the cyclic. With his right index finger, he lightly pulled to a notch we called the first detent, which is for the intercom. Further pressure to the second notch or detent broadcasted on whatever frequency of the radio band was selected, whether it was FM, UHF, VHF, or emergency, which we called guard. All ground troops used FM radios.

The marines were located close to a ridge that stretched for more than two miles. However, they were below the ridge on a cliff that dropped for two hundred to three hundred feet. The steepness suggested the only way to get these guys out would be by rope, which we didn't have on board.

"Black Cat, this is Kilo, over!" Their transmission was weak.

After Lee commented about how low the radio battery was, he keyed and said, "Kilo, this is 2-2. Request smoke."

The marine on the radio responded with, "Smoke's out."

In twenty seconds, a puff of purple smoke hit the tops of some trees about twenty feet above the cliff line but well below the top of the ridge. We had located them.

"Kilo, we copy purple smoke," Lee said.

"Roger the purple."

We had positive ID. Now came the tough part.

There was no way to extract them from their present location. It was so steep that any attempt to get close would result in the main rotor blades striking the side of the mountain or the trees.

"We're all awfully weak from nothing to eat for two days, and our water is gone," came the call.

As we looked for a place where we could extract these guys, Lee said, "They're in the worst place in country for extraction."

Lee told me to fly while he checked out the terrain, and I transmitted, "Wait one, Kilo; we're working on a plan."

A narrow ledge ran along the cliff at the base of the tree line. I don't remember which one of us saw it first, but about thirty yards from the marines, there was a large rock. It was the only clear area in sight. It wasn't even close to being large enough for us to set down because the rotor blades could be into the trees or the side of the mountain before our aircraft could finish its approach.

We still had no idea about the enemy location and didn't discuss it. We just had to assume the enemy was close, and we knew we had to get them out fast. Lee told the door gunners to watch for any enemy activity or muzzle flashes and to open up if any was detected. Muzzle flashes can be seen easily from a klick away. However, in this dense vegetation, the enemy could have been within one hundred meters, and we could not have seen them, or they us.

Lee transmitted, "Kilo, Black Cat 2-2."

"This is Kilo, over," came the same tired voice.

"Kilo," Lee said, "about thirty meters east of your position is a large rock. It's the only area close where we might be able to pick you guys up."

Kilo acknowledged the plan, but with the density of the trees in the area, they had trouble finding the rock. The undergrowth was so thick that their vision was limited to about twenty feet. I kept the aircraft far enough away that I wouldn't hinder their progress with rotor wash. As they worked their way toward the rock, I made a right ninety-degree pedal turn. Lee leaned out the window and pointed in the direction of the rock. Each time we did this, one of them would look up and acknowledge Lee's hand signal. It took more than ten minutes for them to cover the thirty meters.

Finally they all reached the base of the rock that protruded about four feet up with room at the top for one man. Lee told me to bring the ship in as close as possible. The downdraft was strong and gusting, and I wasn't keeping the ship very steady. I eased closer. The right skid was a good six feet from the top of the rock. There was a drop of two to three hundred feet to the ground below. The marines looked at the situation, then transmitted, "Black Cat, what do you want us to do, jump?"

What seemed like a long silence fell over the radio as we all thought furiously. I was having more difficulty keeping the ship at a stationary hover. The distance I maintained was too far for them to jump into the cargo section of our Huey. The marines had backpacks and M14 rifles and were obviously fatigued. I was presenting a moving platform and an impossible distance to leap.

Each man in turn looked down the face of the cliff and then stepped back. I could see them talking among themselves. One pointed up toward the crest of the ridge, as if suggesting they attempt to reach the top, and all three of the others shook their heads. The climb was too steep and would be impossible. The one with the radio, a backpack PRC 25, said, "Black Cat, you're right. It is our only hope of getting out of here."

During his transmission, I backed out of our present position and told Lee that I'd assist the marines out of my cockpit window. I was glad to be off the controls. Lee was fresh and took over, slowly starting us back toward the rock. He had assessed the terrain while I was flying and knew he could get us closer.

Lee held us in a more stable hover while fighting the same strong, gusting downdraft. Our right door gunner left his position and pulled back my side armor plate so I could extend my arm out the window. The outer part of the main rotor blade varied from four to six feet above the marines' heads.

One marine climbed to the top of the rock, the side of the mountain behind him. Lee got closer than I did, reducing the distance to five feet by putting the main rotor blade into the trees, which were three to four feet from the side of the mountain. Small branches started to shatter. The leading edge of the main rotor blade, made of tungsten steel, could take a lot of abuse and still stay intact and flyable.

The first man's eyes were wide with anxiety but under control as he quickly glanced to the bottom below and then looked toward my outstretched arm. He checked his footing as Lee transmitted, "Tell him to jump for the pilot's arm."

The guy on the rock nodded his head as the message was relayed. He began a slight rocking back and forth as if trying to find a rhythm before his leap. With his M14 secured to the rest of the gear strapped to his back, he glared at my arm. He was swinging his arms as though he was trying to jump ten feet. I was worried that his impact with the ship would shake loose his grip and send him falling to his death. What if I couldn't hold him? I may have said it out loud for I heard someone say, "God give me the strength. I can't let these marines down."

I could make out every detail in his face. As he planted one foot, every muscle in his body froze. He took a deep breath and clenched his teeth until his feet left the rock. As he became airborne, his mouth flew open and his eyes widened. Our arms collided and he clung on with a death grip, almost wrenching my arm out of its socket as he connected with the ship. I held his entire weight in the angle between my bicep and forearm. His legs and feet flailed around until one found the skid toe and he was stable.

The sudden impact of extra weight upon the aircraft caused it to jerk sharply down and to the right, bringing the blades down toward the rock where the marine had started.

Lee anticipated this and instantly compensated, pulling away so the rotor blades no longer overlapped the large rock and the remaining three marines. The marine's grip on my arm only increased as the ship moved away. With the helicopter at a hover about forty feet from the ledge, the marine on the skid began to work his way toward the cargo section.

Our door gunner was ready. He had stayed in position behind me after sliding back my armored side plate. When the marine was stable and still attached to my arm, he reached back toward the open cargo section with one hand and clutched the ship through the cockpit window with the other. Our door gunner held his arm out. The marine's left hand then attached to the gunner's as he made his way. At the same time, he gripped the open window and me even tighter as he continued to move ever so slightly back. When he had gone another twelve to eighteen inches, the door gunner was able to grab his backpack and pull him to safety in the cargo section where he rolled safely onto his back.

With one marine on board, Lee maneuvered the ship back into position and the rotor blades rotated over the rock where the remaining three marines waited. The next one looked ready. All three took about the same amount of time to steady themselves and make sure they did not slip off the rock. Each time we hovered into position, they did not take more than ten seconds before they jumped toward the cockpit window and my arm. At five feet ten inches and 140 pounds, I by no means have brute strength, but my arm was going to have to come off before I would let them loose.

Each remaining marine learned from the previous one. The second and third marines' jumps were easier than the first. The last marine almost surprised me when he jumped slightly quicker than the others. Our door gunner had better secured himself in the cargo section and was able to reach out farther to drag each man to safety. What a team effort. We were proud and relieved when the final marine was on board. The recon team was safe and lay on the floor against their backpacks.

We headed for Da Nang. Lee was worn out, and he asked me to fly the ship back to Marble. He lit up a cigarette, and we talked briefly over the intercom. First thing I said was, "Hey, Lee, that was incredible flying. Absolutely great stuff." I looked at him and could not help smiling.

He replied in his slow Southern accent, "Well, I think we all did pretty darned good."

The gunners simultaneously said, "Thanks, sir."

With less than a month of flying combat, there was no way I could have kept the helicopter as stable as Lee did. I had to say it again. "Man, that was some kind of flying."

"He's right, sir," the crew echoed.

The crew chief gave the marines all the water they could drink and offered them cigarettes. The team leader of the recon team asked our crew chief to talk to us over the intercom. He put on the crew chief's helmet and spoke to us, telling us he was glad we came. That sounded strange since there was never a moment's thought of not coming. He then added that for two days the marine helicopters would not come. I never knew why. He told us that they were being chased and were sure the enemy was close. Because of the dense vegetation, the enemy couldn't fire on us. He was sure we had less than five minutes before they arrived. He told us thank you from the other three marines.

We took them to the east side of Marble Airfield. We landed at the closest point we could, which was next to their operations hootch, and were surprised no one came out to greet them. Three of the marines exited in what was obviously total physical and mental fatigue. They did not look back. The team leader leaned forward between Lee and me. We took off our flight helmets as I rolled off the throttle to flight idle. He thanked us again, and he then asked if he could go get us a beer. We kind of chuckled. After all he'd been through, he wanted to get us a beer! We told him to go have one for us instead and that we had some more missions that day. Lee told him that he and his team were some kind of brave, tough marines, and I added, "We're glad guys like you are on our side." He shook both our hands, exited the aircraft, walked about fifteen feet, turned, and gave us a salute. We all returned his salute with respect. I hope they all made it home.

Many times during my tour, soldiers would get my attention after a mission and ask our names to write up a medal. My standard reply was always, "No, that's OK. Negative medal, it's you guys on the ground that deserve all the medals."

Usually they walked a short distance, turned to face us, and saluted like that marine. I can still see each one of them to this day, and it means more than any medal I could have received.

We refueled, switched seats, and flew the rest of the day on resupply missions. I admired Lee. He taught me a lot that day.

−5−

AC ORDERS

I'll be taking over the detachment at Hue soon. It's the further-most northern aviation unit in Vietnam. They've taken more hits and recorded more kills than the entire company combined.

———————————— 7 SEP 67 Letter to Diane

The missions of September 12 started at La Vang, a fairly short clay-packed surface airstrip just west of Quang Tri and ten to twelve klicks south of Dong Ha. The La Vang airstrip was easily recognizable by a wrecked army fixed-winged Caribou at the southeastern corner of the airfield. From here, Lee and I were to resupply Gio Linh, Con Thien, and Charlie 1. They were the outposts that also served as artillery firebases along the DMZ. A firebase could have several 105-millimeter or 155-millimeter artillery pieces, as well as eight-inch guns. They were used to fire into North Vietnam and support any ground operations in their area.

Getting to each location was difficult due to the constant threat of enemy ambushes. We low leveled to each location to avoid observation from the northern enemy artillery. Each outpost could easily be hit. We made radio contact en route to keep each stop less than thirty seconds, and we never shut down at any of them.

In most of the missions I'd flown lately with Lee, I flew from the left seat. Each day I had been in the air indicated to me that it wouldn't be long before I received my AC orders. All of my assigned missions had been purposely scheduled up north into the Hue detachment's AO.

We departed La Vang and headed north at about one thousand feet. When we reached Dong Ha, we quickly dropped altitude and flew low level. I told the crew chief and gunner to fire their M60s into a rice paddy. This made it clear that they and their machine guns were ready. As I got to know the crews better, I would only have to say, "Clear your weapons." They knew exactly what it meant.

From Gio Linh, Con Thien, and Charlie 1, you could see the DMZ. It is best described as a five-mile-wide strip of barren wasteland that separated North and South Vietnam. The Ben Hai River ran through the middle of it. Gio Linh, located on old Highway 1, also known as the "Street without Joy," required the majority of supplies that day. As we dropped down and flew low level, I forced some rice farmers to duck down or scurry out of our flight path since our skids were only two to three feet above the paddies. We then snaked through the sand dunes and bomb craters that surrounded the outpost.

We radioed when we were five minutes from the location, saying "Zero five from your posit," and requested help to off-load the supplies. They asked if we needed smoke to mark the LZ, and I replied, "Negative smoke."

I had been there before and did not want to signal the North Vietnamese that a helicopter was coming. While on the ground in the LZ, we were a prime target for artillery. The craters surrounding Gio Linh were sure signs of the frequency of incoming artillery rounds from the north.

As soon as our crew chief told us that everything was off-loaded, we headed back via a different route to La Vang. We did not draw any enemy artillery while in the LZ, but we knew going back two more times presented problems. The chance of an ambush greatly increased. It gave the enemy time to find cover and prepare for an attack. The North Vietnamese artillery observers would surely be on alert.

Once again, we were loaded up with supplies at La Vang and headed north. We did not climb to altitude but flew a ten-foot low level to Dong Ha to save time. Then the serious flying started once again. I could tell by Lee's body language that my low level had much improved; he no longer stayed close to the controls and was relaxed when I flew.

I took a slightly different route, darting over the rice paddies and then the sand dunes. Up ahead, about four hundred meters, appeared two larger dunes that were six to eight feet high. I started to fly between them when three figures appeared on the top of the right dune, looking like the rifle-range targets at Fort Sill and Fort Eustis during training. I knew we were in trouble even before I saw the muzzle flashes from their weapons.

The time between the muzzle flashes and enemy recognition was probably instantaneous but seemed to take a while. I closed the distance to them going at least one hundred knots. Right after the flashes, I heard their automatic rifles like popcorn popping. But I was committed to the route. Banking left or right or gaining altitude would have only made us a much easier target and given them more time for accurate fire.

Our gunners started to return fire with their M60s. In five seconds, we were going two feet right over the enemy. I banked slightly to the right so our door gunner could get a better field of fire, and at the same time, we flew behind another sand dune and out of range. I felt a tick. We had been hit.

Things were happening quickly. I saw where a round had gone through the right windshield, though no warning light had come on. The door gunners were shooting the entire time, and I assumed had delivered accurate fire on the enemy. But those three men could easily have been part of a larger unit. Going back to re-engage would not be the smart thing to do, so we landed at Gio Linh and gave the artillery fire direction officer the coordinates of the ambush.

There were fifteen to twenty rounds shot at us. The only round that hit us was the one that penetrated the right-front Plexiglas windshield directly in front of Lee's eyes. It passed through the cockpit at an angle between our heads, which were about three feet apart, and then proceeded out the open cargo door. After the artillery officer confirmed the coordinates and apparently prepared a fire mission, Lee calmly said over his intercom, "Let's try a different route out of here."

We shared a quick smile that said it all. Supplying the last two outposts was much easier. The hole in the windshield served as a constant reminder of what could happen. When the missions were complete, we headed home.

After low leveling past Dong Ha, we gained altitude as La Vang passed under us. Lee said, "Congratulations, Bob. You've made AC."

I was surprised he picked that moment to tell me, but I only said, "Really?"

"I'm signing your orders when we get back," he said officially. Then his humor returned. "I want you out of my ship. You're the one wanting to fly up here, and I'll be glad to let you. Just don't bring me again." Lee chuckled over the intercom, but I knew he meant it.

I had to ask, "You think I'm ready?"

"You bet I do. You can handle being an AC."

Instantly I thought of getting my own call sign. I was hoping to get Black Cat 2-1. The Hue detachment commander, Lieutenant Morris, had that call sign and would be DEROSing in two weeks. He had already quit flying.

I said it to myself, "Black Cat 2-1." I liked the way it sounded.

Lee kept his word. An hour after we landed, Major Ward called me in to issue my orders effective the morning of September 13. He told me how important it was to use good judgment as the new Hue detachment commander because I was up there on my own. I gave him my word, confident I would never disappoint him. I had made AC in six weeks. I was very proud, but I remembered how my flight instructor at Fort Wolters had cautioned me not to get cocky, and I promised myself right then that I wouldn't.

On the same orders was my pal W-1 Bart Colburn. I sought him out, and as we shook hands, we reminisced about the three combat assaults we had flown together as peter pilots. We were proud of that as well as both being ACs now. I requested and was given Black Cat 2-1. Colburn asked for Black Cat 2-9, which was Hebert's old call sign. Hebert was going to DEROS in two weeks and was honored that Colburn wanted his call sign.

Major Ward told me to report to supply and draw an M16. As I packed my gear into my duffel bags that evening, several warrants told me how crazy I was for wanting to go to Hue instead of staying at headquarters. They began telling me about the senior advisor at Hue.

Colonel Peter Kelley was a lifer—someone who makes a career out of military service. He had enlisted as a private, worked his way to sergeant first class, and then went to Officers Candidate School. From there he had earned his way to the position of full colonel. The full colonel's rank insignia is a silver eagle, which is a step above lieutenant colonel whose insignia is a silver oak leaf. We referred to a colonel as "full bull," "full bird," or a "bird" colonel.

While they were telling me about "the Prince," as Colonel Kelley was nicknamed, they said how tough he was on his junior officers. I'll have to admit that they were getting me a little worried about reporting to this colonel. I was going to be answering to him on a daily basis. Up to this point in my short army career, I had reported to officers of no rank higher than major. I believed a colonel was the most powerful rank in the army. It is the highest rank that still has personal contact and command over a large number of troops.

An AC from Hue, W2 Jerry McKinsey from Modesto, California, whose call sign was Black Cat 2-4, had ferried down a Huey that needed a periodic inspection. As they sometimes do, McKinsey had with him only the crew chief in the right seat and two door gunners. They were also to pick up the mail for the detachment. I introduced myself and we shook hands. I instantly knew I was going to like him. He knew I was going to be the new commander, and I told him that his reputation of being an excellent combat AC had preceded him. McKinsey stood about five feet seven inches tall, and, even though he looked sixteen, he had just turned twenty. He spoke little and with a slight, almost bashful smile. He was quiet and serious.

This was typical demeanor of ACs who had been in country more than six months. McKinsey walked to the headquarters hootch carrying the M2 .30-caliber carbine that he said had been given to him by the Australian advisors stationed at Hue. He retrieved the mail for the entire detachment and apparently, due to minimum or no conversation with anyone, was back to our fresh aircraft within five minutes. I waited in the middle of the nose of the aircraft out of courtesy and respect for him to select his seat. Without a word spoken, he got into the right seat, leaving the left for me, and we began the start-up procedure. He appeared totally relaxed.

We landed at Hue Airfield, a short two-thousand-foot unimproved asphalt runway with a two-story rundown stucco control tower that was never occupied. Hue Airfield was centrally located within the confines of Hue Citadel, the ancient imperial capital of Vietnam that is of symbolic importance to all Vietnamese.

After shutdown, I was greeted by a veteran crew chief, Specialist Fifth Class Lowell "Dee" Truscott. With a big grin, he said, "Welcome to Hue. This is where you belong, Lieutenant Ford."

I was definitely glad to be away from company headquarters and its protocol.

We drove in a three-quarter-ton army truck made in Japan that was assigned to our unit. We made our way over the Perfume River Bridge, which had been converted from wood in 1906 to a well-made concrete surface with steel girder support. The Perfume River appeared murky and nonflowing as we continued past it toward the MACV Compound. The streets were crowded. Everybody looked busy and didn't pay any attention to us. Bread, vegetables, and all kinds of goods were for sale, including American cigarettes. I saw no presence of American personnel during our trip to the compound. After crossing the Perfume River, we went south one block before turning east two blocks to the front gate of the MACV Compound.

A sign on the gate read, "Unload Weapons HERE!" This meant to take any live rounds out of the chamber but to leave the fully loaded clip of ammo intact. Immediately inside the gate, I saw a two-story stucco building that looked like a hotel. It served as living quarters for the MACV officers of captain and above.

To the left, in the northeastern corner of the compound, was Senior Advisor Colonel Kelley's headquarters. I told McKinsey and SP5 Truscott to "wait one" and with a grin added, "I think it is best I report in."

"Uh, very good idea," McKinsey said. He then looked me square in the eye and said, "Lieutenant Ford, I'm really glad you're here."

"Thanks, I wanted to come."

"No, I don't think you understand. I'm *really* glad you're here." This brief conversation would have much more meaning within two days. I dropped my gear next to the truck, and Truscott said he would stay and secure it.

I did not know if there was a waiting room, so I knocked on Colonel Kelley's door. Almost instantly, I heard a loud, "Enter." There were two men in the room. I took no more than two steps inside and stood at attention. While holding my salute, I said, "Lieutenant Ford reporting as ordered."

Colonel Kelley stood up behind his desk. He looked tough and was about five feet eight inches tall and stocky. He had a ruddy complexion and wore black-rimmed glasses. He returned a quick salute. "At ease. I've been expecting you to report in. This is General Truong."

I glanced at the general. "Yes, sir."

Truong, a South Vietnamese general, was lean and wore freshly starched, faded fatigues with a single white star sewn on each side of his collar. Along with his rank, he had a presence that commanded respect. He was the commander of the 1st ARVN division, which was known to be their best division in Vietnam. He nodded at me without expression. They appeared to be in the middle of an important meeting. Colonel Kelley said very little, but I do remember him saying, "If you do not do your duty as I expect it, you will be replaced. Now go get a haircut and report to the briefing room at 0500."

I saluted and said, "Yes, sir," quickly doing a 180 out of there.

I greeted McKinsey with, "The old man means business!" Old man is a respectful term given to any soldier's commanding officer.

"He's tough on everyone, but he likes all of us," McKinsey said.

Even though I didn't need a haircut, McKinsey pointed me toward the Vietnamese barber where I got a closer cut within the hour.

My hootch was with other lieutenants, all forward air control (FAC) pilots who flew Army O-1 Bird Dog airplanes. These were tandem-seating high-wing single-engine observation Cessna aircraft that were used to find targets and direct fire for artillery, air force jets, naval gunfire, and army helicopter gunships. Every bunk was full, so I took my mattress and put it on the floor. I was getting my things lined out when Lieutenant Morris walked in. I introduced myself. He was cordial and obviously relieved I was there. He told me he had not flown much in the last month. He was due to DEROS in three weeks and was ready to return to company headquarters and get back to America.

One by one, the forward air control pilots came in. Their detachment included five lieutenants, three of whom were Petty, Billing, and O'Shields. Their commander was Captain O'Connell, a West Point graduate who lived in the stucco building. They all belonged to the 220th Aviation Company. They were all good guys who were full of humor. I felt mutual respect from each. Our two detachments would soon develop a close relationship through constant communication during missions.

Lieutenant Morris wanted to get in as much "welcome to Hue" as we could and as soon as possible. Before he introduced me to any of the others, he said, "Let's grab the three-quarter ton and tour the city." I had heard it was off-limits but figured he knew what was secure and could safely be seen.

He took me to the entrance of Hue Citadel, the center of what once was French Indochina or Vietnam. It looked like a scene out of an old *National Geographic* magazine. Ancient brass cannons lined the short path. They were elaborately ornamented and highly polished, clearly well kept, as were the general surroundings. War had not touched this area. There was much pride in preserving the past. We entered through the opening to a simple, well-manicured lawn with a small imperial palace about one hundred meters away. I remember thinking, *All this tour stuff is nice, but I have all year to do this. I'm ready to fly.* I'm disappointed that I never went back to look at this magnificent setting, nor did I return to see the beautiful pagodas, graveyards, and churches that Lieutenant Morris briefly showed me that day. I was so focused on missions and my responsibilities with my men that I never thought of going sightseeing again.

After we returned to the compound, Lieutenant Morris introduced me to several officers who had communication, administration, and medical duties. I don't remember ever seeing them again. Those I do remember meeting and admire to this day were the Australians.

The Aussies—Terry Egan, Ozzie Ostrarrah, Terry Woodell, and my favorite, Desi Ford —were warrant officers in the Royal Australian Army and were advisors to the Army of the Republic of Viet Nam (ARVN) troops just as the US advisors were. Des and I formed a special bond at that moment that still exists. The Aussies were pleased to meet the "new mate in charge of the Black Cats." They were all older, about twenty-nine, and combat veterans. They were sturdy, tough-looking guys in superb physical condition. They wanted me to stay awhile and have a few Fosters beers. I told them I would take a rain check because I had a lot to do, which included meeting all the pilots.

Lieutenant Morris and I started toward the warrant officers' hootch, which was located across a small pathway from ours and also faced the outer perimeter. McKinsey was there with the rest of the men, who had all heard I was in the area. I shook hands with each. The ACs were McKinsey, Al Toews (pronounced "Taves"), and Dwight Dedrick. The copilots were Tom Pullen, Dick Messer, John Aye, and Mark Skulborstad. I told them I wanted to fly with each AC for a day to get more familiar with our area of operation.

McKinsey led the briefing even though Lieutenant Morris was present. He assigned the next day's missions to crews, as well as aircraft they would be flying. He did a good job, and the men accepted their assignments. McKinsey said he and I would fly the next day together on missions that would take us throughout the AO.

I addressed the pilots and told them I was glad to get away from Da Nang and all the protocol. I had to ask, "Any boots or bells to polish here?" That got their attention, and they all grinned as if to say, "He is one of us." I knew it would take a while for us to get to know each other, so I kept everything very simple. No need to give these guys any pep talks. They obviously had proven themselves in combat. I knew that after I flew with each of them, the questions they had about me and I about them would be answered.

When I asked for questions, Dedrick asked if it would be OK to wear our old flight suits around the MACV Compound. Those lightweight, baggy, comfortable air force-type flight suits had been issued to each of us when we first started flight school. They were considered an improper uniform in combat and absolutely forbidden in Da Nang. I told him, "Yes, I'll write home tonight and get mine sent to me." I could tell I was going to like these warrants.

I started for my hootch to organize my personal gear and write a letter home. My letter was going to start with what I had promised Dedrick. I was relieved that these guys felt the same way I did about strict protocol and that they already were comfortable enough with me to ask about the flight suit. Lieutenant Morris headed toward the officer's club, but as I was about to enter my hootch, Pullen got my attention.

"Lieutenant Ford," he said, "one more thing." I returned to the warrant hootch. "There's a little problem," he said. Pullen, the oldest of the bunch at around twenty-six, started the impromptu meeting. "Two gunners were caught by the MPs for going to an unauthorized location in Hue."

I figured what that meant and was right. Pullen had taken it upon himself to talk to the MPs and get the gunners released, but the gunners needed to hear what I had to say. Pullen and I went to their living quarters in the southwestern part of the compound. He introduced me, and I told them I had heard of their reputation as being the best gunners in Vietnam. I knew they had volunteered for door gunner duty after serving a one-year tour in the infantry. They had asked to serve at Hue because they knew they could get daily contact with the enemy.

I said, "If you guys get caught again, I promise I will send you to Da Nang, and you both will finish your tour pulling guard duty, KP, or in maintenance." I added that I would write to their mamas and tell them what happened. For these two hard-core combatants, that would be more humiliating than being locked up, and I knew it. I never heard of them getting caught again.

I got to my hootch and went to the latrine. I was brushing my teeth before showering and enjoying the very cold—about forty-eight degrees—water when I looked above the old, stained porcelain sink and saw in bold letters NON-POTABLE WATER. I had just about begun to drink the stuff. I stepped into the shower and there was only one knob there too for the same forty-eight-degree water. I learned quickly to get wet in five seconds, step out of the shower and soap down, and then bear the frigid water for ten to fifteen seconds to rinse off. It wasn't too bad when it was over.

At four-thirty, I woke to the distinctive metallic ping of a Zippo lighter. Lieutenant Billings had an early takeoff and was lighting his first Lucky Strike of the day. By four-fifty, I was in the command briefing room, standing off to the side like a new guy not wanting any attention. Colonel Kelley took charge immediately and asked for detailed information from all officers present. He asked questions in machine gun fashion, one after another. If he did not get a quick, clear, precise answer, he would raise his voice and ask the same question again, followed by, "Now do you understand?" He was tough on everyone. Those who did know the answers to Colonel Kelley's questions still had trouble putting them into words due to his intimidating manner. He demanded that his advisors be prepared for their missions and keep him informed; he stated this over and over.

Colonel Kelley started to break up the briefing, but then he looked at me, pointed, and said, "That's Ford. He's now in charge of the Black Cats. I'm sure you'll get to know him. OK, that's it. Any questions? If not, dismissed."

I liked Colonel Kelley's direct manner. He wasn't as tough as my high school basketball coach, but he was close.

Lieutenant Morris had been on the radio and told Da Nang HQ that he was going to bring a helicopter down for maintenance. He left that morning, and I never saw him again. I got his bunk, and I felt in charge. I knew I was going to like the warrant officers. They were so much like the warrant officer candidates I had been around my third and fourth month of flight school.

Four or five days later, after our nightly meeting, McKinsey said, "Lieutenant Ford, we decided not to call you 'Sir' or 'Lieutenant.' We all think it should be 'Boss.'"

"OK, sounds good," I said.

Walking to my hootch, I knew it. This was where I belonged.

–6–

FOX 4

I think I'm going to like it here. There is much more responsibility for a detachment commander. The flying up here is better. You have to do much more low level because we're so close to the DMZ. They have opened up many more free fire zones. The VC are getting much more aggressive. Besides engaging the enemy and going on CAs and regular supply missions, nothing out of the ordinary.

—— 10 SEP 67 Letter to Diane

Tom Pullen and I dropped off some personnel at Quang Tri and refueled hot, topping off 1,250 pounds of JP-4 fuel with about 190 gallons, making us good for about two hours of flight time. We were on our way south to Hue for another mission supporting the South Vietnamese Army. I enjoyed flying with Tom. He had been an enlisted soldier for five years before flight school, and he had a calm, "old" sergeant look to him. He was always the first to find the humor in any situation.

Over the UHF, the emergency frequency, we heard, "This is Crown on guard." Crown was an Air Force Lockheed EC-121 Warning Star, a four-engine propeller aircraft that provided navigation and assistance for combat search-and-rescue missions.

"Any ship in the vicinity of Yankee Charlie, go blue."

I gave Pullen the controls and said, "You got it."

I got my Signal Operation Instructions out of the pouch located on the outside of my chest protector just below my chin. "Tom, fly a heading of 225 degrees toward Yankee Charlie grid square."

All other radios were turned down to prevent interference with the next transmission. Pullen cranked it up to over one hundred knots as I urged, "Let's go!"

While I turned the pages in the SOI to find the blue frequency on UHF, I hoped this SOI was current. I dialed in the frequency next to blue, one of fifteen colors for designated frequencies, and hit the transmit button on the floor. "This is Black Cat 2-1 up blue, do you copy?"

Crown responded, "Roger, 2-1. Location of two downed PAX. Are you ready to copy shackle?"

PAX were passengers and shackles were codes to identify locations, so I got out my grease pencil to copy the code on the windshield. "Roger. Copy. Wait one," I said, indicating I'd be back in less than a minute. I translated the shackle into grid coordinates from my SOI within thirty seconds, marked my map within a 1,250-meter grid square with a black dot, and then responded back. "This is 2-1, one five from location."

I was not going to let these guys on the ground stay one second longer than necessary. We were on our way.

I took the controls back from Pullen and visualized our route, noting landmarks as well as the point where we would cross the A Shau Valley. Having marked the approximate location, I laid the map on the console and corrected the route that I was hoping would lead to the spot on the map.

I put the ship on the deck, five to ten feet above the top of the jungle canopy, while Pullen took the map to get oriented. The trees under our skids were a blur. We were now moving at 110 to 112 knots. I was sure glad we had no passengers and plenty of fuel.

The door gunners were told to make sure they had a fresh belt of ammo. They had already reloaded their M60s, and in five seconds both of them fired a short burst. They had been listening to all radio traffic and were ahead of me and ready.

We crossed A Shau Valley, which was solid enemy-controlled territory, and were headed for our destination—now a mere point on the map that I so hoped was accurate. Everybody was silent, waiting for what would happen next.

Crown transmitted, "We are scrambling cover for you."

That probably meant A-1 Sky Raiders would work to cover the extraction. At this moment, the downed pilots' wingman excitedly transmitted, "I am staying on station for cover."

Since we were rapidly approaching the designated location, I did not acknowledge either transmission. Three minutes later, I said, "Crown, this is 2-1, getting close to location."

"Roger, 2-1, we have voice communication of both downed PAX."

After I slowed to forty knots, I felt my grip tighten on the controls. All my senses were 100 percent alert. I spotted a clearing ahead and dropped into it as our ground speed slowed to a stationary hover. We all looked for any movement.

"Don't fire without positive enemy ID or muzzle flashes," I cautioned.

We strained to see a downed pilot as we hovered for about thirty seconds, though it seemed much longer. We knew the enemy would be scrambling to any open clearing knowing the pilots would do the same.

"2-1, our PAX can hear you. You are close," Crown transmitted.

I exited instantly, keeping about the same heading to bring us into another clearing. The next clearing I could see was three hundred to four hundred meters ahead of us. It was about the same size in area as the first one but narrower. I immediately slowed while descending and prepared to land. Just as the skids cleared the top of the jungle canopy, a pen flare went straight up to our right no more than fifty meters away. I landed and thought to myself, "My God, we found him."

We fast hovered toward the pilot to meet him halfway while he ran toward us. I set the Huey down within ten feet of him. Then he stopped and drew his weapon, a .38-caliber revolver, and turned back toward the jungle as if to fire on any approaching enemy. I could not believe what I was seeing and yelled at Payne, my door gunner, "Get that guy on board!"

I knew the enemy had to be close, but we couldn't fire until we knew the location of the second pilot. Payne exited the aircraft and ran up behind the pilot who was still aiming toward the jungle. With a bear hug, Payne lifted then carried him back to the Huey and tossed him on board. While Payne plugged himself back in on the intercom and repositioned behind his M60, I looked at the pilot. He had scrambled up on his knees and was right between Pullen and me frantically pointing toward the ten o'clock position. I knew what he meant: his partner was in that direction.

We did not fire our weapons. I pulled in full power to exit and proceeded in the direction as he kept pointing. He was literally between our two heads in the cockpit. I never got over forty knots and within one klick spotted another clearing.

For the third time, the wingman above called again and asked if we needed cover. I was irritated because he interrupted my concentration and responded, "What kind of ordnance do you have on board?"

"Two five-hundred pounders."

"Negative five-hundred pounders, out."

The rescued pilot yelled loud enough for us to hear, "I think this is it! I think this is it!"

We were flying fifty feet above the jungle canopy to give the guy on the ground a better chance to see us. Crown came up, "Your PAX hears you. Close." After a slight pause we heard, "Have you in sight."

I approached as fast as I could, following what I thought would be the pilot's line of sight from the only clearing in the area. As I was landing in the clearing, still light on the skids, the second PAX came running toward us out of the darkness of the jungle no more than twenty meters away. I watched over my right shoulder as he dove into the helicopter and his momentum carried his head and shoulders out the other side of the cargo section. The first PAX and our crew chief and door gunner, Thomasson, grabbed a handful of flight suit and pulled him back into the Huey. But our relief was short-lived. Being a single ship in enemy-held territory is never good. My gunners immediately started firing at any suspected enemy location as I pulled in all power and exited low level out of the clearing.

I flew low level through the top of the jungle, which slapped the skids every second. I said to myself, "Keep flying, you beautiful aircraft. Keep flying." We stayed low level as we headed for the nearest friendly area, which was Phu Bai. We crossed south of the A Shau Valley heading approximately ninety degrees. After about fifteen minutes on the deck, I made a rapid climb to twenty-five hundred feet. Pullen dialed in Phu Bai ADF, a pre-set beacon frequency, to confirm our location. With relief, I called Crown, "Both PAX safely aboard. I say again, both PAX safely aboard."

We were proud, and Crown responded with, "Good job, 2-1. Stay up this frequency."

Pullen and I both figured Crown wanted us to stay on this frequency until the mission was completed, but we were wrong.

Thomasson told me one of the rescued pilots wanted to talk to me, so he gave the guy his helmet and showed him the thumb transmit button. He quickly said, "I'm a lover not a fighter."

I replied, "Really, OK. You are also alive."

The bravado subsided and he added, "Hey, thank you, guys. You saved us from a miserable rest of our lives if we would have been captured. We could hear rifle shots, some automatic really close. They would have been on us within two or three minutes."

Hearing that made me proud of my navigation, and I asked, "What kind of aircraft were you flying?"

"F-4 Phantom."

"We call you guys FOX-4s or fast movers," I said, but I wanted to stop the conversation and get Thomasson's helmet back on him. The crew chief is your eyes on the entire left side of the aircraft, and I felt uncomfortable not having him hooked up to the intercom. I asked the pilot their base location and he told me Da Nang. I checked the fuel gauge and said, "Good because Da Nang is the only air force base we could have reached without refueling. We'll take you home."

Thomasson got his helmet back on, and I said over the intercom, "Hey, you guys, did you hear the wingman say he was going to cover us with five-hundred-pound bombs? How's that for close support?"

I'm sure he was excited and wanted to help, but those bombs probably would have blown all of us up. We all chuckled and made a few comments about the wingman. Realizing we were still up on the blue frequency, I called Crown, "Crown this is 2-1, taking both PAX to Da Nang main. ETA four zero."

I didn't get a response from Crown and was getting ready to switch frequencies when Crown came up, "Black Cat 2-1, say again your last transmission."

My short reply was, "En route to Da Nang, over."

During fifteen seconds of silence, we were expecting a positive thanks. Instead Crown transmitted, "Black Cat 2-1, proceed with PAX to Quang Tri."

I thought that was a strange request. I was now closer to Da Nang than Quang Tri. I delayed for a minute then responded, "Crown, say again?"

Almost apologetically but with sternness, Crown said, "You will proceed to Quang Tri at this time."

I pressed the intercom transmit and said, "You know what I think? The air force wants to take these guys back. We can't let that happen after all of this."

"We're with you, Boss," Pullen said, with Thomasson and Payne echoing, "We're with you, Lieutenant."

"OK you guys, if we are ever asked, back me up on my next transmission," I said, then transmitted back to Crown, "Crown, this is Black Cat 2-1. Unable to copy. Be advised you are coming in weak, broken, garbled, and distorted. Switching to Da Nang main frequency at this time," and then emphatically, "OUT."

We deserved the satisfaction of taking them back. Tom switched to Da Nang main, and within ten minutes we radioed the tower, "Da Nang main, this is Army Huey, one five from your position with two PAX on board."

"Roger, Army, report at zero five."

Five minutes out, I radioed, "Da Nang main, this is Black Cat 2-1, zero five from your facility for landing instructions."

It was obvious that after the wingman arrived at Da Nang, he had told everyone, including the tower controller, about our successful mission. The controller radioed, "Black Cat 2-1, you are cleared via direct in front of maintenance hangar." Then he added, "Welcome home!"

"Roger, Da Nang. Five hundred feet over Da Nang Bay. You should have me in sight."

"Roger, 2-1. No traffic. You are cleared to land."

On short final approach, it looked like everyone at the base was moving toward our Huey. As soon as we were firmly on the ground, the crowd approached the cargo section and picked up the two pilots, carrying them as men would their new brides until they cleared the radius of the main rotor blades. I reduced the RPM to flight idle while this took place. At flight idle, the 1,100-horsepower turbine engine as well as the main and tail rotors are at about 55 percent power with the main rotor blades spinning at 250 RPM compared to 380 RPM when at full throttle in flight. At idle, there's much less noise. After clearing the rotor blades, the rescued pilots each got a ride on the shoulders of two or three of the other pilots. They never looked back. They were carried to what appeared to be their operations hootch.

A lieutenant colonel was left standing alone right outside my window. I assumed he was their wing commander. He held two bottles of Canadian Club whiskey and started to hand them through the cockpit window. I took off my helmet and gave him a salute and asked him to give the two bottles to my gunners. Even at flight idle, I had to raise my voice to be heard. "Sir, these guys save our butts every hour. They deserve it."

He walked back and presented Thomasson and Payne the whiskey and then returned to jump up on the skid toe once again. He wanted our names for a write-up.

"Negative write-up. Glad to help. Besides we left some unfinished missions. They have been calling. I gotta get back." I got closer, about six inches from him, and yelled, "Sir, let's all try to get home and make babies."

He smiled in obvious agreement, shook his head, and raised his voice over the noise to say something to the effect of, "You army pilots are something. We all know what you're like. Good luck, son."

He reached in and put his hand behind my neck in a fatherly way before we shook hands. He jumped down off the skid, walked out about thirty feet, turned to face us, and popped a crisp salute, which we all returned. We knew we had all done well. A salute from this impressive air force officer meant a lot to each of us.

During the rest of my tour, when any soldier jumped on the skid toe and wanted to write us up for a medal, I always repeated, "Negative. Let's just get home and make babies." It always brought a smile and a salute from them after they walked in front of our Huey. From the aircraft, their salute was returned with respect.

I got takeoff clearance from Da Nang tower and flew the three-minute flight to Marble Mountain for fuel. We did not take time to report to Company HQ and refueled again hot—just as we had a couple of hours before.

After takeoff, as we were just north of Hai Van Pass, Lieutenant Petty, whose call sign was Cat Killer 2-4, came on guard. "Black Cat 2-1, this is Cat Killer 2-4, come up uniform."

I dialed in our predesignated UHF frequency for general conversation and said, "Hey, 2-4, this is 2-1."

Petty asked our ETA to Hue.

"Three, five minutes. What's up?"

"I've got a unit in contact that needs help. Sure could use you. Contact them on Jack Benny minus 2.3."

We used the "Jack Benny" reference several times every day, which referred to his permanent age of 39. It was simple, fast, and always worked.

"We'll be there in three zero," I said, dialing to 36.7 on the FM radio.

"Let me know when you are zero five," Petty said, adding that he'd monitored our entire rescue. "You guys did a great job. You earned your $120-a-month flight pay."

—7—

DAILY CHALLENGES

Everybody carries an M-16 in the helicopter. I sometimes carry the M-79 grenade launcher. You know war can be really funny. Not a day goes by that something doesn't happen that's actually funny. I love your letters. Put some perfume on them.

====================== 13 SEP 67 Letter to Diane

Enemy activity began to increase. Every time we pulled medevacs or resupply, enemy gunfire was more frequent and intense, especially north of Dong Ha. Whenever we refueled at Dong Ha, we followed the standard procedure to call their Petroleum Oil and Lubrication (POL) frequency to determine if any aircraft were in the area or incoming. During refueling, it was common to have incoming enemy artillery in the area, so we expedited the refueling process as best we could. The pump at Dong Ha was the slowest of any POL location.

One time, we put in only five hundred pounds of fuel to keep the total fuel on board under nine hundred pounds and keep us light. We were supporting a major ground operation close to the DMZ. We visually cleared ourselves before exiting, and I pulled in power along with forward cyclic to prepare for low-level takeoff back to the operation. We were about four feet off the ground with minimum forward ground speed when the engine suddenly quit. I leveled the aircraft, executed a hovering autorotation, and softly set it back on the ground. What had happened? We had gone no more than ten feet from the refueling point. If the engine had quit even two minutes later while low leveling in enemy territory, survival would have been difficult.

I asked the crew chief to check things out. This was not a good situation for a stalled aircraft. We made a good target. I put out several calls on the POL frequency to attempt to advise them that we were shut down due to an unknown mechanical problem, and after at least three minutes, I got a response.

"Black Cat 2-1, be advised of a possible fuel contamination."

Fuel contamination? That could be anything. I had never encountered this problem. I knew that if I could get a radio relay to headquarters at Da Nang, it would take a minimum of four hours to get maintenance personnel here. Not knowing what kind of contamination, I asked the crew chief to drain some fuel out of all seven sumps underneath the aircraft. Maybe we could identify the contamination.

Crew chiefs normally carry a small clear-glass jar to check the fuel for water. Water is heavier than our fuel, JP-4, and can easily be observed in the bottom of a jar of fuel. The first sump he checked was underneath one of the fuel cells. He showed me the contents.

"Lieutenant Ford, this is either all JP-4 or something else," he said.

We all looked at it, dipped our fingers into the contents, and while rubbing them together smelled the liquid. We readily confirmed it was almost 100 percent water. I said, "Open up all the sumps and let them drain. Check it every minute to determine if we are getting any JP-4."

I called Cat Killer forward air control and told him to relay our situation to one of my men. We did not want to spend the night there, and troops needed us. He called back and said the other two aircraft were on other missions but could divert and head our way in case of emergency. Dedrick and McKinsey were fully engaged in support of ground operations at different locations.

With the battery switch on, I observed the fuel gauge at nine hundred pounds. We estimated we had five hundred pounds of contaminated fuel. We were not sure what the textbook solution was, but we needed to try something. After draining all seven sumps for twenty minutes, the fuel indicator went from nine hundred to five hundred pounds. When we checked the liquid coming out of the sumps, they indicated 100 percent JP-4—no water in the jar. After waiting five minutes with the sumps closed, we checked each one again. We still had 100 percent JP-4. We conducted a standard startup procedure, and the turbine responded normally. We kept the engine at full RPM for five minutes. We had no idea if a pocket of contaminated fuel was still in the system threatening another engine failure.

Over the intercom, I said, "OK, the troops need us." I made a decision to fly to Quang Tri to refuel. All of us agreed that our sense of duty to care for troops on the ground was stronger than our desire to be cautious and stay shut down until a maintenance crew arrived.

We flew at eighty knots two thousand feet above ground level in case the engine quit again so it would be easier to autorotate to a forced landing area. I kept Cat Killer informed so he knew where we were in case we went down. We refueled at Quang Tri and flew four more hours that day, completing our missions without incident. I worried the entire time about another engine failure. I hoped I'd made the right decision to fly the Huey, and, as it turned out, I had.

The Huey was a remarkably reliable aircraft. It was rare ever to have maintenance problems with one. Other than stopping for routine or scheduled inspections, the daily efforts of dedicated crew chiefs kept them problem free with little downtime. But there was an occasional problem.

Once we encountered a starter exciter not wanting to cooperate. Starting the aircraft was more difficult with each attempt. The next day, we solved the problem by not shutting down after the first start. We flew all day and went directly to maintenance in Da Nang as our last stop. The exciter was replaced, and we were on our way back to Hue that night.

Early in October, we flew all day in Crew Chief Joe Sumner's aircraft. I began to feel a slight catch in the tail rotor pedals. The catch felt like pulling a cable through a smooth tube with a loose or broken strand on the cable. Each time through, I could feel a tick or slight pause affecting the smooth flow. This happened every fifteen minutes. By midafternoon when we were refueling at Hue, the tick occurred every two or three minutes. I had mentioned it to Sumner when I first felt it, and now I was very concerned.

Joe was the typical first-rate crew chief. He started to investigate. He unscrewed several plates on top of the cargo section to inspect the push/pull tubes for smooth, free movement. We checked everything for fifteen minutes while at flight idle. He inspected all critical parts he thought necessary as I moved the tail rotor pedals full travel, hoping he could visually find the problem, but we did not feel the hesitating tick. We concluded it must happen only during full RPM. Before rolling the throttle to full RPM, we told the passengers and door gunner to stay clear of the aircraft. Joe stayed in the aircraft right behind the armored seats.

Even at full RPM though, we could not feel any tick or hesitation. I decided to take it up to a three-foot hover while Joe inspected under the plating again.

When I applied the left pedal to keep the aircraft in a stationary hover, it would not move. I pushed as hard as I could with my left foot to keep the Huey from spinning to the right to follow the torque of the main rotor blade. *Surely the pedals would free up*, I thought, but they didn't. In those two or three seconds, we had already spun one and a half times. I looked up, and everything was a blur. During the next two seconds, I remembered flight school and emergency procedures for tail rotor failure. One procedure was to attempt to fly the aircraft out by pulling in more power, then eventually streamlining the Huey in flight. This was impossible because there were obstacles all around. I had no way out.

The other procedure was to roll off the throttle and settle the aircraft back on the ground. I started rolling off the throttle while trying to keep the horizon level. I knew when the spinning aircraft settled to the ground that both skids must hit simultaneously or we could flip over. If the main rotor hit the ground at its 550-MPH rotating speed, the entire aircraft would become a twisted mess and probably ignite into flames and burn like a match head. I'd seen it happen.

Everything was still a spinning blur. As I continued to roll off the throttle, I felt the skids begin to scrape the ground. I applied a slight left cyclic. The inside skid started to take more of the impact. If the outside skid took more impact, it might catch on an object or uneven ground and flip us.

With most of the weight now on the skids, the aircraft started to slow its spinning. It was a wild, dusty ride. I had stayed close to the same spot during the entire episode. Everyone had scattered, and nobody was hurt. I was glad that I had instantly recalled what I learned in flight school. Sumner thought we had spun four or five times in the air and twice after making contact with the ground.

"I think we should call the maintenance guys from Da Nang on this one," Sumner said with a slight smile.

"Good idea. I don't think we want to go through this again," I said.

Later we found out that the tail rotor servo had quit because the directional valve had frozen. After the valve was replaced, the aircraft performed beautifully again.

Another subject covered in flight school, if only briefly, was vertigo. We were warned that continually transitioning from visual flying to instrument flying could quickly cause severe vertigo. When these conditions occurred, if not corrected quickly, it created a life-threatening situation for the entire crew.

Once when flying at fifteen hundred feet and trying to find a troop location, we encountered low-lying clouds that temporarily obscured the ground. We had them pop smoke but couldn't see it. I was positive we were close to the unit on the ground and decided to go lower. At one thousand feet, I looked down and still saw only patches of ground. Then we flew into another cloud. On my third attempt to focus on another small area of ground, thin clouds moved under us, obscuring everything. I felt dizzy and decided to cross-check the flight instrument panel.

The instruments indicated a normal reading, but the aircraft felt as if it were trying to go to the right. The next thing I did or said had to be absolutely correct. Instead of counteracting with the flight controls, which my mind told me to do immediately, I calmly said to my copilot, "Johnny, when was the last time you flew instruments?"

"Gosh, Boss, it's been a while," he answered.

"OK. Just for the heck of it, maintain this altitude and fly a heading of 090. You've got the aircraft."

"Sure, Boss, I've got it. I always liked flying instruments."

In my mind, the Huey was now starting to experience severe vibrations and was even more severely flying back and to the right. I felt as if we were becoming inverted.

As calmly as I could, I asked, "How are things going?"

"Going great, Boss. This is fun."

I was totally disoriented and as screwed up as Bill Grogan's goat. I knew if we flew at 090 toward where our flight originated, we would break out of this low-lying scud. I told the door gunners to be part of this short instrument flight and to let my copilot, W1 John Aye, know when we were completely clear of the clouds and they could see the ground. It was all I could do to muster up a clear voice.

In five minutes, they announced, "I see the ground, sir. We are out of the clouds."

"Thanks, men. Good job, John," I said. "Why don't you fly us over and get some fuel? You make the call and tell them we're inbound."

"Go get some fuel, Boss? We still have about eight hundred pounds."

"Go ahead. It'll be good experience for you to handle it all by yourself."

The cockpit was still a spinning mess to me. I knew the best way to come out of vertigo was to have clear sight of the horizon, which we now had all around us. Still it took me more than thirty minutes to get over that confused state of mind. I didn't recover until I was out of the cockpit while we refueled. Walking around, I finally began to feel like myself.

When I got back in the cockpit, the Huey's instruments and controls looked and felt normal again. I was finally and thankfully OK. I did not tell the crew what I'd experienced. I just started back and completed several more missions.

After this incident, whenever I found myself in similar flying conditions, I had my copilot fly on instruments before vertigo could take hold. I wondered how many pilots and crew members had been killed as a direct result of vertigo.

—8—

VICTOR ZULU 1-4

I have one less week in Vietnam. It may seem like the wrong attitude, but this has never stood in the way of the U.S. doing its job. I swear there are more heroic deeds done in one day over here than I thought existed in a whole entire year. Things aren't all bad. It seems you can always find something to laugh at. Tell everybody hi. Also advise all to stay away from Vietnam for any winter vacation plans.

— 30 SEP 67 Letter to Dad and Bill

I held nightly meetings with all the pilots in the warrants' hootch for routine assignment of aircraft and missions to crews. I would include locations of units in the field and contact radio frequencies.

I listened in to the details of our previous day's encounters from the other ACs. It was a good practice to trade narratives of the day's events. Each mission was challenging, and diverting for emergencies or using our judgment to fly a more important mission was routine. The ACs led the recount of missions, and the pilots added their input. Every night, we could have written a chapter of a book on what we saw and did.

We very seldom saw one another during the day. We were "single ship," supporting Vietnamese with their American advisors, marines, and US Special Forces. This took us daily throughout the area of operation in support of those who needed us the most. Once, while refueling at Cu Viet, a marine major jumped on the skid and yelled, "Son, do you know how important you Black Cats are to this war?"

Since we never wrote up one another for medals, we enjoyed giving "attaboys" for any missions that were extra challenging. There were several of these nightly. We all got big laughs when in unison we went through the routine of saying to the recipient, "OK, ready, one, two, three—attaboy!"

I met separately with the other three aircraft commanders—McKinsey, Dedrick, and Toews—to talk about each copilot's progress and any concerns about crew chiefs or door gunners. They always had high praise for each.

We were required to report to company headquarters in Da Nang on the Lima Lima, phonetic for L-L, which was what we called the telephone landline. It could take thirty minutes to get an open line, so I would pick up the receiver and instantly declare, "Operational emergency." This was a made-up term, but when I identified myself as the 282nd Assault Helicopter Detachment commander, it always worked.

I handed the phone to the newest pilot, W-1 John Aye, to give all the reports. Aye, whom we had nicknamed Baby Son because he had the boyish face of an energetic thirteen-year-old, had a good gift of gab and willingly accepted this responsibility. He kept everything brief and simple. If he was questioned, he didn't answer but said he would get back to them later. Since Aye did not have direct accountability for the reports, he was seldom questioned.

One day, Dedrick hit a duck while low leveling, and it came through the Plexiglas chin bubble. It made a mess, and the chin bubble had to be replaced. Aye asked me how to report it, and I told him to tell headquarters that the aircraft had sustained a hit from an enemy B-1-rd.

He was not questioned until two weeks later. An intelligence officer from battalion headquarters got on the line during Aye's report and wanted a detailed account of what type of weapon was the B-1-rd. Aye covered the phone and asked, "What do I say, Boss? This is a captain."

I told him to have the captain write down B-1-rd, wait until he did, and then tell him we hit a bird. The captain fell silent for a moment and handed the phone back to the company clerk for Aye to complete his report. After that, Dedrick's nickname became the "Dangerous Duck."

At least every other evening at approximately 8:00 p.m., I reported to Colonel Kelley. I stayed in uniform during my nightly briefings so I could be front and center with the colonel within five minutes of any request to appear.

I would report with a knock on the door of the command hootch, and Colonel Kelley would yell, "Enter!" I'd give a crisp salute and say, "Sir, Lieutenant Ford reporting as ordered."

Colonel Kelley always followed with an "at ease," and he would immediately ask a series of questions about the day's events. He wanted to know the specifics of what we observed in the field of combat operations such as enemy strength and details about those in command positions. Commanders could include Vietnamese, special forces, marines, Australians, or any army personnel under his command. I admired them all and always passed on my compliments to Colonel Kelley about their bravery and coolness under any enemy condition. If we diverted from our primary mission, he wanted to know the circumstances and why. Even though this happened many times, he wanted a briefing of each occurrence, which I always suspected was only confirmation of what he already knew.

This review of specific incidents could take some time, and he knew it. He knew me well enough to know that I was prepared to tell him every detail truthfully. He admired our independence and our daily contact with the enemy. We thought he would have occasionally liked to be one of our door gunners. When I would get to the details of a mission, he often stopped me in mid-sentence to say, "OK, that's enough. Go write a brief report. No copies, in pencil, put it under my door," followed by, "You're dismissed." My reports were typically written within an hour, and I was never questioned about any of them.

There were a few times, however, when he wanted all of the details about a diverted emergency. He listened intently as anyone would to a good war story. On one such mission, we had left passengers at a friendly outpost before reaching their final destination. We were diverted by forward air control to fly medevacs, resupply, and close-fire support all day for another combat unit that was in enemy contact in another area. Colonel Kelley apparently had already been told that we had many medevacs and resupply missions that day. Our door gunners were given credit for more than seventy enemies killed in action (KIA) while providing suppressive fire during the last part of the operation.

After he dismissed me, I saluted and started to leave his hootch.

"Was McKinsey involved in all that?" he asked.

His question threw me for a split second. Colonel Kelley had never asked about any of my pilots specifically by name. My instant thought was to protect my men and take the blame if there had been an unfavorable report, but I had never been evasive with any answer.

"Yes, sir, he was."

"He's a real pistol, isn't he?" Colonel Kelley said with a slight smile.

"Yes, sir, he is," I replied with pride.

On December 18, 1967, I had assigned myself to a mission to take care of a unit that had been in the field for a week. We had already gone to their position twice for resupply. Each time en route, we switched to the frequency that Desi Ford was using. He was the senior advisor in an ARVN unit in an operation ten klicks southeast from where we were located. All Aussies were designated Victor Zulu. His call sign was Victor Zulu 1-4.

Desi looked tough and weathered, and he moved with the efficient movement of a trained athlete but he was by far the most humorous of all the Aussies. He always remained cool-headed. Desi had become a close pal, and I told him we would monitor his tactical FM radio frequency on a regular basis any time he was on a combat operation just in case he needed us. It was routine for us to call a forward air control in our area after checking on Desi to see if we were needed for any emergency. Since we were diverted regularly, this resulted in flying an average of two to five missions an hour.

Desi's radio operator, SP4 Bailey, was a strong soldier from Little Rock, Arkansas. Their respect for each other was obvious. After receiving my call, Bailey would hand the PRC-25 radio receiver/transmitter to Desi, and he would always joyfully say, "Thanks, mate" or "Thanks, Fordy, for checking in." It was always good to hear that Australian accent.

It had been over an hour since our last communication. I dialed in his frequency and transmitted, "Victor Zulu 1-4, this is Black Cat 2-1." There was no answer. The frequency on the FM control panel was confirmed and all was correct, so I repeated my transmission. After a seemingly long pause of ten seconds, Bailey shouted, "Black Cat 2-1, Zulu down, Zulu down!"

Within seconds, we were headed toward their last known position maintaining one thousand feet. Whatever the problem was, Desi needed us. I radioed back, "Zulu 1-4, this is 2-1. Zero five from your position, be ready to pop smoke at 02. What is your enemy condition?"

"Roger, 2-1," came the reply, "taking some enemy fire three hundred meters from a tree line north of our position."

Everyone in the aircraft was monitoring all the radio traffic, but I checked by asking if all had heard the transmission and got two clicks from each door gunner. We were going in hot. They would be ready. In four to five minutes, I reported that we were two minutes from the approximate position and requested smoke. Within thirty seconds, we spotted the smoke and corrected our route.

"I've got purple smoke," I said.

His radio operator quickly said, "That's us! That's us! We hear you!" Then after a slight pause, "Have you in sight."

I landed like we did many times every day—fall from the sky, lose altitude as fast as possible, don't over speed the main rotor, and pull in full power to stop the rapid descent within three feet of the smoke grenade.

As we landed, the right door gunner opened up. He was using solid tracers in his M60 to cover the tree line with accurate fire. I searched for Desi and his radio operator to my front and left and saw fifteen to twenty soldiers in defensive position but nobody moving toward the aircraft. None of the soldiers was returning fire to the tree line, so I knew there was no immediate danger.

"Cease fire," I said. "Do any of you guys see any wounded?"

"Someone is coming toward the aircraft carrying a wounded soldier," said the crew chief.

As I leaned forward and looked over the armored seat to the left rear, I saw my pal Desi carrying a Vietnamese soldier. The insignia on his collar indicated he was a major. He was unconscious, and his uniform was covered in blood.

Right before Desi put him in the cargo section, I glanced at the major and thought he was dead. Why had the radio guy yelled "Zulu down"? Confused, I watched Des carry this soldier to the aircraft. Des laid him behind me on the cargo floor, and I looked down and to my right into the face of the Vietnamese officer. His lifeless form and the dark shade of purple in his face confirmed my thoughts.

I wasn't sure if there were any more medevacs. I glanced out the cockpit window, expecting Des to jump up on the toe of the skid to give us a report on any more casualties and enemy conditions. He wasn't there. At that instant, someone pulled on my right sleeve, and I looked back around. Des was two feet from me, inside the helicopter. I could barely hear him over all the noise.

"Fordy, you got ten minutes," Des yelled.

The look on his face told it all. Only then did I see his uniform was soaked in blood from his waist to his knees.

"Are we clear?" I asked instantly over the intercom. "Coming up!"

Both gunners reported back clear, but I was already pulling in power. Increasing power to the main rotor, I made a pedal turn to head the aircraft toward Phu Bai. Within seconds, we were at full speed of approximately 105 knots.

"Tom, put me up Phu Bai Tower," I said before transmitting on their frequency. "Phu Bai Tower, Black Cat 2-1, one zero northeast from your facility. Request via direct to hospital pad."

The hospital pad was in the middle of Phu Bai but south of the runway. Staying clear of traffic by going around to the east or west would take well over a minute—time I felt we did not have. The tower operator called back, "Negative direct, we have traffic in the area."

I came right back, "Phu Bai this is 2-1. Zero seven with medevac request via direct."

We never got over five feet off the ground. All the power was pulled in, and we were on course and closing fast.

The tower operator came back, "2-1, cannot clear you across our active at this time. We have too much traffic."

We were only three minutes out and needed help, so I transmitted emphatically, "Phu Bai, put your six on." That meant I wanted to talk to his commander, hoping he was in the tower and monitoring all of this.

"2-1, this is Phu Bai six," the commander instantly transmitted. "Are you declaring an emergency?"

"Affirmative emergency," I said.

"You are cleared via direct. Break, break. All aircraft in the vicinity of Phu Bai make a go around. All aircraft on the ground hold your position and standby," he transmitted.

I thought to myself, *I did it! Des has a better chance.* "Roger, Phu Bai, have medics standing by."

We were almost there. In twenty seconds, I was shooting across the middle of the airport. It was all I could do to get the aircraft stopped within thirty feet of the hospital. The tower had notified the hospital, and medics were standing with stretchers in hand. Des gave me a thumbs-up while he and the major were being loaded onto the stretchers. Des looked bad, in the first stage of shock, but we had easily beaten his request of ten minutes.

I called the tower. "This is 2-1. Request clearance for takeoff."

"Roger 2-1. Expedite out the same way you came in."

As the main runway zipped under us, I quickly got to full speed while maintaining two to four feet. I transmitted with feeling, "Phu Bai six, 2-1, thank you, sir. We're clear."

"Glad to help, 2-1. Break, break. Be advised all traffic in Phu Bai pattern the runway is open. Report your position."

Tom changed the frequency back to the last unit we were supporting, and we were on our way back north.

"Tom, sure hope Des is OK," I said.

Tom looked over and smiled as he lit up one of the Salems his wife sent him fresh from the States. "I think we saved his tough Aussie butt to fight another day," he said.

In ten minutes, we had climbed up to one thousand feet and then made contact with the unit we had left. We gave them our ETA.

I keyed the intercom, "Hey, Tom . . ." He knew me well. We had flown over four hundred missions together, and by midafternoon he knew my five-year-old C-ration cigarettes were tasting stale. He anticipated the rest of my sentence. Instead of answering, he lit two Salems at the same time and handed me one. Sometimes he would hand me two unlit ones and say, "Here, Boss, take two in case we get separated."

Whenever I had trouble lighting a cigarette in the cockpit with the old C-ration paper matches, which was often, Tom would reach over with his Zippo to light it. He would then announce over the intercom to the gunners, "Make your way up here and pat the lieutenant on the back to help him get this thing started." I could always hear the laughter throughout the aircraft even over all the noise.

Later Des told me he only remembered the speed we flew and never getting over two feet off the ground as he held one bloody testicle in place the entire flight. His other had been shot off, but it didn't keep him from fathering a child after returning to Australia. I had been wrong about the Vietnamese major. He survived but lost both legs. Des thought he was an excellent officer. On December 22, just four days later, Desi returned to the MACV Compound. He was one tough Aussie for sure.

For Christmas, all the Black Cats gave Desi an old softball with our names and hometowns written on it. We thought this gift would substitute for what he had lost. He was back leading a combat operation by mid-January. Of the hundreds of soldiers I medevaced during my tour, Desi Ford, Victor Zulu 1-4, was the only one I personally knew.

—9—

A ZIPPO AND GOING FEET WET

I've been doing the usual flying, no real thrilling experiences—at least not to me—lately. I didn't think I would be the type to get used to seeing and flying dead people, but I am. I guess I don't write about what I'm doing much anymore. Sometimes it's a rotten job, but mostly rewarding.

————————— 20 OCT 67 Letter to Diane

We flew late into the evening. My copilot was John Aye, the one we'd nicknamed Baby Son. The ground unit released us at about eight o'clock in the evening, and all was secure. We had provided more than an hour of close, accurate, suppressive fire. Earlier in the day after the troops had been resupplied and all medevacs and KIAs extracted, we asked if they needed any extra firepower from our two M60s. We received an affirmative. The ground units were always appreciative of the offer. Even though we knew the location of the enemy, we confirmed it again with the CO.

Our door gunners were ready. We started at about one thousand feet firing at known or suspected enemy locations while covering the entire area with accurate fire. We then came down closer—four hundred to five hundred feet. Many times, empty casings from our expended rounds would land on friendly troops, hot but harmless. When this happened, we got panicked radio calls. They thought the brass casings were bullets from our M60s.

We gave the guys on the ground quite a show and, more importantly, weakened the enemy—we were given credit afterward for many enemy KIA. We had flown three days and into the night supporting a major operation against a large North Vietnamese Army (NVA) unit. It was the farthest south of the DMZ of any major encounter with the NVA. Our support was the turning point of a successful operation, which made us proud.

On our way back to Hue when we were flying at fifteen hundred feet, the ground commander called. He said a reconnaissance team from his unit that had been out for three days needed to be picked up. He gave me their approximate location, and I visualized the open terrain and elevation. We had flown all over this area for the past two days. The commander was in radio contact with them and estimated the team was three or four klicks from his main element.

By now, it was dark. I had flown at night many times, but I had not flown a medevac or an extraction this late. The extent of my night flying was going back to our base after a mission, a five a.m. takeoff, or a firefly mission.

We received the FM frequency of the patrol and made the call. Their radios were strong. I hoped they were within ten klicks of our aircraft. When they responded with "Black Cat 2-1, we copy," we had already turned on the FM homing course indicator. I asked for a short count. Heading their direction, we kept our navigation lights on steady dim to keep from attracting attention. With lights on bright steady or flashing, an aircraft is an easy target.

We headed toward their location at twelve hundred feet flying eighty knots. We knew they could hear us long before they could make visual contact. In three to four minutes we heard, "You're coming our direction."

I slowed to sixty knots, acknowledged, and then asked, "What is your enemy situation?"

"Not sure. Probably all around us within one thousand meters."

The FM homing course indicator showed we were slightly right of course. I maintained this course so they would be on our left side—my side. In two minutes, we got a response: "Real close." I asked if they had visual contact of our aircraft, and the answer was "Negative."

I asked Aye to switch the navigation lights to bright steady. In ten seconds came, "I see you." I asked them to confirm color. There was a slight pause, then, "Red." All aircraft have red navigation lights on the left, green on the right, and white on the tail. The FM indicator gave me verification. I was close. My plan to make the pickup was going well.

"I need to ID your location," I said. "Give signal."

"All we have is a Zippo lighter."

During ROTC boot camp at Fort Sill, we had seen a demonstration of a soldier lighting a cigarette a mile away. We were amazed how we could pick up the tiny light. Remembering this, I knew we could see a cigarette lighter in this environment. The small flash from the lighter looked like a muzzle flash from a rifle but stayed constant. I set up a basic simulated traffic pattern to land for the extraction and we switched the navigation lights back to steady dim.

Keeping the flicker from the Zippo on my left and using my peripheral vision, I flew an abbreviated downwind losing five hundred to six hundred feet during the crosswind leg. We were set for a closing descent. Slowing to forty knots on our final leg, I kept the touchdown point—the Zippo light—in the windshield. I knew the light would start to climb up the windshield during final descent.

"Landing lights, Boss?" Aye asked.

"Negative. Too good a target and will mess up our night vision," I said. "Not sure of the enemy."

In any tough situation, you do things by the numbers, so I repeated a process of checking altitude, airspeed, closing speed, ground speed, and touchdown point. There was no other outside visual reference, so I kept the small flicker of light just left, then just right of the center of my eye. In flight school, we had been told never to stare at an object because it will start to move within the blind spot located in the back of your retina. This can give a pilot the illusion that a stationary object is constantly moving and cause you to change the aircraft's flight path incorrectly when you shouldn't. The results can be disastrous.

As I descended and the soldier's flame started to rise on the windshield, I simultaneously slowed the aircraft. Everything seemed to be working.

"Any visual contact?" I asked my men over the intercom. They all responded, "Negative."

We had to be close. Slowing the Huey even more, I was sure we were within twenty feet of the ground and twenty meters from the soldiers. I gradually descended, closing the remaining distance. The light was no more than ten feet in front of us at eye level.

"I see them," one of the gunners said. "They're right here!"

At that instant, I could make out the form of a face in the glow of the flame. We were about a foot off the ground. Either the rotor wash blew the flame out, or the soldier shut the cover on the lighter as he came around the nose of the Huey. They all loaded up in the cargo section as our skids lightly touched the ground. One of the soldiers grabbed my shoulder and yelled, "All on board." I made a standard takeoff as if on instruments. After climbing to fifteen hundred feet, we checked in with the CO of the operation and told him his men were all safely on board.

"Thanks, those are good soldiers," he said. He told us to take them back to Hue. Men from his unit would be waiting.

Before the reconnaissance team exited the aircraft, one of them reached forward and gave us a thumbs-up in the light of the instrument panel. We had flown more than ten hours and fifteen missions that day.

After shutdown and post-flight inspection, I was tired. We all were. Later during my tour, I flew several night medevacs and extractions. Each time, the soldiers had a handheld strobe light or an army-issued flashlight. The Zippo had worked just as well.

I met briefly with all the pilots in their hootch for mission assignments. When I started to leave, I turned around and said, "Flying in Vietnam at night is like flying up a pig's butt."

Everyone agreed. Aye was sitting on his bunk looking as exhausted as I felt. "That's a good description, Boss," he said without looking up.

Everything had turned out OK. It was a solid, rewarding day—as most were.

I recall another rewarding day that began at 6:30 a.m. as we loaded supplies and planned for a seven o'clock takeoff for an emergency resupply in bad weather. A small unit close to the Laotian border had been without food and water for two days. During my tour, the most desperate-sounding radio transmissions were from soldiers on the ground when they had run out of water. The lack of visibility would make it difficult to get to them, and the forecast wasn't improving. They were on top of a mountain. The forward air control working the area told me everything was completely engulfed in fog except for two or three mountaintops, one of which was the unit's location. He had made both visual and radio contact. Getting to them was going to be a challenge.

We were socked in with less than a quarter mile of visibility. It would be impossible to low level west through mountainous jungle terrain. I called Cat Killer to check if a possible landing area was still open on the mountaintop. He confirmed, but it would be necessary to climb through the clouds to about twenty-five hundred feet to get there. I was confident I could get to the soldiers, but getting back could be a real problem.

Before taking off, I came up with a plan. I knew we had to have a known location to navigate back, so I called a ground unit we had supported the previous day. They were in the cleanup phase of their operation, so I asked if they were still in the same area that I had marked on my map. They were, so I asked them what kind of visibility they had. They confirmed about a quarter mile. I asked them to continue to monitor this frequency because we would be calling back in forty-five minutes.

I told my copilot to look out of the cockpit and tell me when we cleared the clouds. I did a standard instrument takeoff, and at two thousand feet he reported it was starting to clear and get brighter. I told him to make certain we were completely on top before I got off the instruments. Continually trying to transition from instruments to visual outside contact in marginal weather risked inducing vertigo. We would operate visual flight rules, called VFR, once on top of the clouds.

At twenty-four hundred feet, he told me we were well above the clouds. I looked up from the instruments to observe a magnificent sight. The sun was behind us, and as far as you could see spread a solid blanket of white. This was a first for me. I took a picture of this incredible, tranquil scene and thought, *This must be what heaven looks like.*

I averaged taking about one picture every two days. I was able to take them when shut down in a friendly LZ or when I felt comfortable having my peter pilot fly the aircraft at certain times, such as flying straight and level between missions or into a landing zone for at least the third time after it had been secured. The developed photos came back as slides, so I sent them home.

After five minutes, I saw two mountain peaks barely penetrating the clouds and hoped that one of those was our destination. I estimated when we were three minutes out and called to verify their location and instructed them to pop smoke. With no wind, the smoke engulfed the landing zone.

The last fifty feet of the approach to the small LZ was straight down. With heat, high altitude, and the weight of the cargo, we had only one chance to make a safe landing. We were much too heavy to make a go around. The door gunners made certain the tail rotor remained clear of the trees and thick bamboo during our descent by telling me to turn slightly left or right. If the tail rotor spinning at 1,660 RPM hit an object, the aircraft could spin out of control. We safely touched down.

After unloading the needed supplies, we were much lighter. The troops gave us thumbs-ups, and we easily climbed out of the LZ. Then came the tough part.

We headed back, still VFR on top. After about ten minutes, I called for the confirmed location of the ground unit and asked for a weather report. He said visibility was less than a half-mile. The only way to get back was to make an instrument approach to the troops on the ground using the FM homing course indicator. When the radio operator with the unit began a long count, I set up a standard instrument approach and started descending through the clouds. I told my copilot to look forward and down to verify when there was visual contact with the ground. I knew if we broke through the clouds short or long of the troops, we would be OK.

The terrain for two kilometers around their location was mostly flat and almost sea level. That gave me the confidence to go Instrument Flight Rules (IFR) and fly an instrument approach. My copilot was to tell me when he first had sight of the ground and to continue talking me through the final stage of the descent to one hundred feet off the ground. As the radio operator gave me long counts, we continued a standard instrument approach. My copilot did a good job. He waited until he saw the ground and gave me a quick update. When he declared we were one hundred feet above the ground and clear, I looked out and stopped our descent. We made it. Experience, confidence in my crew and aircraft, and a strong desire to take care of the soldiers had produced a successful mission. It was a good feeling. Although we never made visual contact with the ground troops, I thanked them, switched frequencies, and proceeded to refuel.

While refueling, I saw a well-respected marine major whose duty was to serve as a liaison for navy, marines, and the Vietnamese Army. We had flown him to different locations in our area of operation several times. He asked me to take him to a ship sixteen klicks or ten miles offshore in the Gulf of Tonkin. I always looked forward to doing different things, and this was a first. I didn't like to fly far over water and out of sight of land, which we called "feet wet." He showed us the ship's location on the map. I thought, *How tough can this be?* Landing on some big boat could be fun. From our altitude, we could see at least five miles out, so finding a ship in a grid square should be a simple affair. I told him to climb aboard, and we headed out over the water.

The only ship in the grid square was a landing craft utility (LCU) ship about 135 feet long with a small landing pad where our skids would barely fit. To make the landing more complicated, the ship was traveling south, and the wind was coming from the east. The ship was rocking constantly from side to side at least twenty degrees each way.

We made the approach to within five feet of the pad. The back-and-forth movement made the deck appear above us, and then disappear. The third time it started to disappear, I forced the Huey firmly on the landing pad. From the cockpit, the side-to-side movement of the ship seemed severe. The aircraft's nose and tail were now moving up and down forty degrees. We were looking first at the sky, then the water. The major jumped off and disappeared.

I asked if we were clear. I was ready to get off this thing. My crew chief yelled, "Negative! Negative! They have lashed us down with ropes."

The ship's crew must have thought we were going to slide off backward into the ocean. So did we. Before I could say anything, the major jumped back on and said, "This is the wrong ship."

He had another location and frequency for us and pointed north. I brought in enough power to get the weight of the aircraft off the skids. As soon as we were untied and the nose of the ship started to come down, we jumped off the deck. After climbing to one thousand feet and heading toward the second ship, we called the designated frequency. We estimated we were five minutes from their location and requested landing instructions. The major got the intercom headset we sometimes carried and told me that this was a much-larger ship that was equipped to carry helicopters and smaller propeller-driven aircraft. The navy approach controller asked what kind of aircraft we were, who was on board, and if I had a TACAN, which is a radar-identification instrument.

"Army UH-1, negative TACAN," I said. "I am four minutes off starboard for landing instruction with a code seven."

I was proud that I'd come up with a navy term—"starboard." I wasn't sure a major even had a code, but that sounded important, and

I was trying to make a point with the guy. Among the pilots, we used "codes" to quickly identify VIPs. Code one would be the president of the United States; code two, a four-star general, code three, a three-star general; and code four, a two-star general.

After I announced I had a code seven on board, it took a minute to get a call back. The control tower operator said he had me in sight, and, after a slight delay, with slow, dripping sarcasm he said, "Be advised, army. You are off port side."

Even though he was right, my pride wasn't going to take this navy remark, so I said, "Be advised, navy, I am landing via direct. Keep all personnel clear."

We landed as far away as possible from all other aircraft. We didn't see any sailors. The major jumped off, went out in front, and gave a quick salute. He had heard the interchange and gave me a smile and thumbs-up. I called the control tower.

"Any aircraft in the vicinity? We clear for takeoff?"

A quick "Affirmative clear" was the response.

I landed only one other time on a ship, the hospital ship *Repose*. I went to visit a Cat Killer roommate, Rick Billing, who had taken a glancing blow off his flak vest from a .51-caliber while flying recon at two thousand feet above Quang Tri. It took a six-inch chunk out of his shoulder. The unique thing about the trip was that we were permitted to shut down. No incoming wounded in action (WIAs) were expected. They invited us to lunch, and we enjoyed the silverware, china, white linen tablecloths, and wonderful food, including ice cream. The hospital personnel never stopped asking questions. They all wanted to hear about the war firsthand from army pilots. My copilot, Mark Skulborstad, wolfed down everything in front of him while I fully answered each question. It was difficult to enjoy the meal through all the talking, but I understood. The crew of the *Repose*, as well as the other hospital ship, *Sanctuary*, performed a magnificent service for us.

−10−

CREW, LOCALS, AND A DUSTUP

I received the tape recorder. I don't know if I'll send tapes or not. All I could talk about is what happens over here, and no one wants to hear war stories all the time. Better go. Have a mission.

— 14 OCT 67 Letter to Dad and Bill

During my first six weeks in country, I had admired how the aircraft commanders made so many decisions in a day without mistakes. They made it look easy. From preflight inspections for the first flight to filling in the logbook after the last missions, every decision made was entirely on their shoulders. When flying single ship in combat, these decisions were even more numerous. To a new guy in country, even radio transmissions were complicated. Aircraft commanders were confident and did this with ease. ACs regularly communicated with forward air controllers and cleared the aircraft through artillery firebases, naval gunfire, B-52 strikes, and high-performance aircraft unloading their ordnance. It took timing and precision. ACs very seldom took part in unnecessary or idle conversation during any mission. They constantly cross-checked flight instruments for normal readings, planned every minute for an area to land in case of an emergency during flight, and maintained proper intervals in formation during combat assaults.

Other decisions that demanded no mistakes involved navigation and knowing how an aircraft would perform fully loaded in all kinds of LZs under enemy conditions. That's what we called "being ahead of the aircraft." The aircraft commander just did not have time to include the crew in these decisions.

When I became an aircraft commander, I transitioned into that responsibility and continued to improve. By the time you made AC, you had already proven yourself to your commanding officer, unit standardization pilot, and, most importantly, other aircraft commanders. You were ready for the decision-making responsibility, or you would not have received your AC orders.

I occasionally had fun with my crew by telling them I wanted to include them in making what we called a "command decision." I would say, "I want all you guys to help me on this situation." They would not say it, but I knew what they were thinking: *Really?*

"Here is the deal," I told them one time. "The twenty-minute fuel warning light came on five minutes ago."

As I pointed to the warning light panel, they rose up from their door gunner positions, turned, and looked to verify. The copilot glanced down to his left.

I said, "Let's all decide what we should do." Laughing inside, I waited for someone to state the obvious.

After some hesitation, one of them said, "Well, sir, we should go get some fuel."

"If everybody agrees, then that's what we'll do," I said. I was already headed that way, of course.

When we were two minutes out from the POL refueling station, I'd tell them, "Remember, you guys helped make a command decision today."

They realized I had set them up, and we all had a good laugh. Each time I pulled off this gentle ribbing, it made our crew a closer unit.

I also enjoyed teasing our hootch maid, Pham Thi Bon. The hootch maids were hired from the local civilian population after passing security checks. They were assigned to different hootches to keep things clean and orderly while we were fighting the war. The Cat Killers and I had the oldest maid in the compound. We also joked that she was the oldest woman in Vietnam. Pham Thi Bon was the sweetest, kindest, most-talkative Vietnamese person I had been around—even though I could understand little of what she said.

I didn't see her very much because we were always flying. When I did, I made it fun. In front of other hootch maids, I picked up all seventy-five pounds of her and told her I was taking her home with me. Through her smile, her teeth stained purplish-black from chewing betel nuts, she said something that sounded like "Troung wi dinkee dow," which meant, "The first lieutenant is crazy." Then she pointed to my wife's picture and said, "She number one."

I would then point to Diane's picture and say, "She is number ten. You are number one. I take you home today."

The more she shook her tiny, bony finger at me, the more the other hootch maids laughed. I usually ended it by saying, "I not take you today. I take tomorrow."

"OK, OK!"

It was entertainment for all of them.

One day when I was in the compound, they invited me to share their lunch. We all ate bamboo shoots, seaweed, and slivers of some kind of meat with a small rice ball seasoned with nouc mam. Nouc mam is a rotten-smelling sauce made from fermented fish heads and sea salt. It tasted like bone marrow to me. I think I was the only American they invited to have lunch with them. Before our lunch broke up, I asked one of the gals who spoke excellent English to ask another lady who spoke no English to imitate me as I was talking at that moment. When she did, it was as if my voice had been recorded on 78 RPM and played back at 33 RPM. I was amazed how our English sounded to them, so unpleasant and groaning.

A month later, in front of about seven of the civilian lady workers in the compound, my little elderly hootch maid presented me with a sixteen-inch round linen table covering. She had beautifully hand-stitched a floral pattern surrounding a deer in delicate precision. She had included four embroidered doilies with three cats on each looking at a mouse around a fringed circle. She was so proud to have given me such a beautiful gift that she had spent hours creating. After she presented them to me, she neatly folded and placed them in a linen pouch that she had precisely decorated with an embroidered pond scene with ducks paddling around water lilies and cattails. As I gave her a hug, all the ladies smiled and politely clapped. Later, in private, I handed her twenty American dollars.

I still treasure Pham Thi Bon's gift as much as I do her memory.

However, there was an individual who crossed my path whose memory I do not hold quite so dear. I could tolerate a lot, but one thing I would not allow was disrespect shown toward my men.

On this particular day, three crews left the MACV Compound at 5:00 a.m. and headed to the airfield in a three-quarter-ton truck. Two aircraft had an early 6:00 a.m. takeoff in order to be on station for two operations. No emergency had been declared, but the troops on the ground always needed us. The third ship had to go to Da Nang for a periodic inspection. Dedrick and Messer were to leave the ship and immediately fly back in a fresh aircraft.

We were all doing our walk-around preflight when Dedrick said, "Boss, if I run into Lieutenant Olstin [not his real name] again, you may have to testify at my court martial."

"What do you mean?" I asked.

"Well, I knew you would be mad if I told you what happened. But I thought I should say something now in case I run into him again."

I walked over to Dedrick. "All right, what's up, and who's Olstin?"

"Well, Boss, two weeks ago, you sent me to get the mail and a fresh ship, and this Lieutenant Olstin stopped me on the flight line over by the operation hootch. In front of our crew and several other warrants on the flight line, he yelled, 'Hey, Mister, don't you warrants know how to salute? I know you're from the Hue detachment, and you are going to salute superior officers around here.'" I felt that even though a lieutenant outranks any warrant officer, he should show respect for those warrants who had been in country much longer and flown hundreds more combat hours.

"Olstin did that?" Dedrick was easygoing and never complained; he was always smiling and friendly with everyone. When he told me about this incident, I took it seriously. "You take my mission. I'll go to Da Nang."

"Now, Boss, I probably shouldn't have told you."

"No, I'm glad you said something. I'd like to meet Olstin, and I'll take care of it."

I stayed calm most of the way to Da Nang, although the thought that Dedrick had to take a chewing out from a new in-country lieutenant started to renew my anger. We reported inbound to Marble Mountain and then switched the frequency to operations. I asked if maintenance had a specific revetment to leave the aircraft or if I should land directly in front of their main hangar. Maintenance was ready for us. Our fresh ship along with its crew chief was standing by ready to leave. As we went through shutdown, the door gunner started to take both of our M60s to the other aircraft. I told Messer to get the mail.

"Don't waste time—help the crew get everything ready to go," I said. "I'll be back. I won't be long."

I left my chest protector on and grabbed my M16. I asked Messer to take my flight helmet to the other aircraft and headed for the platoon hootches. I could feel myself getting angry again. I knew I was not going to like this guy. I stood in the door of the first platoon hootch and asked, "Is there a Lieutenant Olstin here?"

Total silence.

I looked around. There was only one lieutenant in sight. He had a mustache and was smoking a pipe, not saying a word. Now I knew I didn't like him.

"Are you Olstin?"

"Yes, I'm Olstin," he replied. He then puffed up and demanded, "Who are you?"

"I'm Lieutenant Ford from the Hue detachment. I want a quick word with you outside."

He walked behind me as we went about twenty-five meters toward the parked aircraft. Then I turned to face him. "Let me tell you, you chicken, no-flying SOB," I said. "If you ever dress down any of my men again, if you ever make them stand at attention and salute you, if you ever talk to them again, I'm splitting you apart. Now, if you say anything back to me, I will take you down."

I looked him straight in the eye, paused, and then turned and walked away. I was too mad not to make good my threat. I walked directly to the ship where Messer and the crew were waiting for me. I believe it was good that no one heard my outburst, though Messer had seen me talk to Olstin and asked what I'd said. I told him that I had a friendly chat with the lieutenant and had asked him to be a little nicer to our pal Dedrick, as well as to all the Hue pilots. My voice was calm, but I was still steaming inside.

"I think we need to get you back to Hue," Messer said, smiling.

We took off immediately, and I noticed the fresh aircraft had a vibration. This happens when the two main rotor blades, each being twenty-four feet long and weighing two hundred pounds, are not perfectly in track or alignment while at full RPM. At 340 RPM, even when slightly off track, that creates a vibration throughout the Huey. I've flown many hours with the blades slightly out of sync. Voices become distorted. The blades must follow one another perfectly through the air to eliminate the vibration.

Hoping it would smooth out, we continued to fly another five minutes. It got much worse and became so bad that we could not read the instruments. Our voices were barely audible. We had to go back. I called operations, and by my voice they knew what was wrong. Someone made a good decision and had another fresh ship ready for us.

When we landed, there was no sign of Olstin. I looked for him from the cockpit. I doubt I was the only one who had experienced this problem with him, but I may have been the first one to call him out on it. I never regretted showing my anger. I felt validated. My men would not be humiliated or shown such disrespect. That was the only dustup I had with another officer during my tour.

We returned to the Hue airfield and shut down. One of our ships was already in a revetment. It was unusual, but everyone in the detachment was there except the crew of the third aircraft. Within ten minutes, the third Huey approached. Dedrick was the AC. While they were at flight idle preparing for shutdown, I had an idea and briefly told everyone before I jumped on the skid toe to tell Dedrick.

"Go back up, fly outbound for five minutes, then come back low level from any direction going ninety to one hundred knots," I said.

I wanted to find out if we—or the enemy—could determine the direction of an inbound Huey flying on the deck. We had taken very few hits when flying at low level given the amount of gunfire directed at us. Within five minutes, we heard the familiar popping of the Huey's main rotor blades as Dedrick approached.

I asked each pilot and crew member, "OK, from what direction is Dedrick coming?"

As we answered, Dedrick shot ten feet over us and was out of sight in five to seven seconds. Three of the ten got it right, and they admitted they were guessing. I missed it by ninety degrees, confirming that the enemy just didn't have time to react until we were out of sight or out of effective range of their weapons. We flew low level even more after this experiment.

–11–

VIP MISSIONS

The news magazines sure have been misinformed. I haven't read anything yet that agrees with what I thought happened to General Hochmuth.

================================= 17 NOV 67 Letter to Diane

None of us wanted to fly a VIP mission. A VIP to us was any rank of a full colonel and above. When assigning the VIP missions, I distributed them equally among the ACs. Even with all the respect we had for Colonel Kelley and General Truong, we did not enjoy flying them to meetings. Although they were important to the war effort, these missions took us away from the war and the satisfying thrill of flying combat. On VIP missions, we had time schedules, and we flew standard takeoffs and landings like we did in flight school. There was usually a lot of boring ground time. However, when we flew north of Dong Ha, flying low level was a tactical necessity.

There was one humorous thing Colonel Kelley often did. After saluting him and General Truong upon their arrival at the helicopter, Colonel Kelley gave me a quick inspection, pull out thirty-five cents of military payment certificates, and hand them to me with instructions to "get a haircut." We were always sharp in appearance, but it was his way of letting me know who was boss while having fun at the same time. We all believed it was the father in him. He couldn't help correcting his boys, even if there was nothing that needed correction.

When commanding generals from other units requested a flight in our area of operation, I was often requested by name. However, when assigning missions at night for the next day, I attempted to push those missions to another AC. After they thought about it and realized who was going to be the passenger, the other ACs—Dedrick, Toews, and McKinsey—would stop me in midsentence while I was briefing them and say, "Whoa, wait a minute, Boss. Did you say general?"

"Yes, why?"

"Because they want you, Boss."

They had been around long enough, and there was no way I could fool them. Actually I felt honored to be selected to fly these high-ranking officers. They shouldered enormous responsibility.

The first VIP mission we flew was the commanding officer of the 101st Airborne, Brigadier General Barsanti. We picked up Barsanti and his aides at Phu Bai and flew north to the area where the 101st was going to relocate. The recon included the area around Camp Evans along Highway 1. He treated me no differently than he treated his aides, which was abrasive. Instead of talking on the intercom with the provided headset, he firmly tapped on my helmet or pushed on my shoulder, then pointed the direction to fly. I was glad when he left the aircraft. I saluted him when he first arrived, as well as when he exited. He returned neither salute.

In early November 1967, I received orders to pick up two-star Marine General Bruno Hochmuth at Dong Ha and take him and his party to Khe Sanh. We picked them up at the marine complex close to where we regularly refueled. We proceeded low level to Khe Sanh as we always did—paralleling Highway 9-West. The terrain was mostly jungle and enemy territory. Upon arrival, the general was obviously irritated and yelled, "Why did you fly so low?"

I explained it was safer because there had been heavy enemy activity, as well as reports of heat-seeking projectiles. We always flew low level this close to the DMZ. He still seemed unnerved, and he probably would have chewed me out some more except he had several marines waiting for him. Since we had been dismissed, we took off as soon as he cleared the rotor.

Over the intercom, I told Tom there was something I wanted to try. Our Cat Killer buddies had told me that if you low leveled through the A Shau Valley, you could surprise the enemy, and they would not have time to direct fire toward you. He couldn't remember if anyone had actually done it, but it kind of made sense. Just think how exciting low leveling through the strongest-held enemy territory in South Vietnam would be? We thought it would work, so we decided to try it.

We headed south, picked up the north end, and descended into the A Shau Valley. We flew about ten feet off the deck. We found a trail that eventually spread out into a well-worn road, and we eased back to eighty-five to ninety knots. Everything was going as I thought it would. I knew we were flying through hundreds of enemy soldiers, but I was surprised we never heard gunfire. Every fifteen seconds, we flew over twisted metal on both sides of the road that looked like some destroyed mode of transportation. We flew by Ta Bat, A Luoi, and A Shau, which had remnants of a packed dirt runway and parts of aircraft. We distinctly saw the body of a banana-shaped Army H-21 Shawnee over on its side. The whole valley looked like a salvage yard.

Tom dialed in the Phu Bai ADF preset beacon frequency, and when we cleared the valley, we soon could see Phu Bai east of us.

"We made it," I told Tom. "That was fun. Let's go back."

"Not this time, Boss," he said, smiling.

Instead we went to get fuel, reported our location, and headed out on another mission.

On November 14, 1967, Tom and I were again flying missions in bad weather with only a half-mile to a mile of visibility and a four- to five-hundred-foot ceiling from Phu Bai to all points north. While we stayed low level paralleling Highway 1, we saw a Marine Huey and one or two Marine H-34s flying in the same direction over Highway 1 but at least thirty knots slower and about one hundred feet higher than us. We commented to each other that they must be inexperienced because flying at that altitude and slower speed left them exposed to enemy fire.

Three hours later at 3:00 p.m., we were refueling hot at Dong Ha when we received a call on guard.

"This is Cat Killer 2-6. Any Black Cat come up uniform."

While still on the ground, we dialed in our predetermined frequency on the UHF. "2-6, this is Black Cat 2-1." Cat Killer 2-6 was the Cat Killers' commander, Captain O'Connell.

"2-1, I thought you would be the only one flying in this weather. I need you to go to the south side of My Chanh. There's a helicopter accident. Possible shot down."

"We are on our way."

We found the wreckage quickly and were ready for any enemy. We didn't take any enemy fire and noticed a few ARVN soldiers standing casually around the wreckage—a Marine Huey. Tom and I commented that the fuselage, although over on its right side in about three feet of water, looked intact and without fire damage. The main rotor blades were bent but had little damage. The transmission had been torn from the airframe and lay nearby. With that degree of damage, the Huey couldn't have been at much altitude or had any ground speed upon impact. The tail section was still intact and attached to the cargo section.

I called 2-6 and told him what I had seen and asked if there were any medevacs.

He radioed that there was one code four—a two-star general—killed in action, and a marine ground unit had taken care of security. We saw one body bag resting on a rice paddy dike. I told 2-6 that papers were scattered across an area about the size of a football field. Tom and I thought we would stay in the area to see if we were needed and decided to check out the papers. We soon saw an SOI and some papers with "Top Secret" stamped across the top. Our two gunners reluctantly got out and for the next fifteen to twenty minutes, gathered up most of the papers in waist-deep crud. Thomasson got stuck in the mud, and we hovered over to him. He put his arm around the skid and freed himself. Back in our Huey, he and Payne were a smelly mess. With all the papers secure, I asked 2-6 where we should take all of this. I also asked about the body bag. He responded, "Take the papers east of Marble Mountain to Marine HQ in Da Nang."

I received no response about the KIA, so I assumed it was probably an ARVN soldier.

A few days later, it was confirmed in the *Stars and Stripes* military newspaper that the code four killed in action at My Chanh was Major General Hochmuth. Later I read it was a possible tail-rotor gearbox malfunction. Whatever the reason, we lost a marine general that day. He was outstanding, as they all were.

Early in December, I had my third VIP mission. When I met Lieutenant General Robert Cushman, the commanding general of all marines in Vietnam, I knew I was in the presence of a great leader. When he arrived for his flight, I stood at attention as he returned my salute and then shook my hand. He gripped my arm with his left hand and said, "Son, you have been selected to take me to two firebases on the DMZ. I have been told that if anybody can get me there and back safely, you can. Do you have any instructions?"

I immediately went from a state of awe to combat flying mode. "Sir, when we get to Dong Ha, I will fly low level to the two firebases. I do not want to attract enemy artillery from the north. When we land at both places, you will have seven seconds to exit the aircraft. When you call for pickup, I'll come from a different direction, and you will have seven seconds to get on the aircraft after the skids touch down."

He listened intently. He then turned to his aides and asked if they had any questions. Their eyes were focused on me as they all responded, "No, sir."

I flew him right on the deck, never higher than ten feet. At two minutes from the landing zone, I called inbound to let them know we had a VIP on board, a three-star general: "Black Cat 2-1, code three, negative smoke."

At Con Thien, they all followed my instructions. Within five seconds, my door gunners said, "We're clear." I pulled in power to exit, glanced to my right, and saw the four marines had almost covered the distance to the command bunker. These locations were extremely familiar to us as we had been there well over twenty-five times. We did not need smoke to mark these landing zones. The exit route I chose was close to the same route we had used coming in.

I got back to Dong Ha and got a call saying that the general wanted to be picked up in ten minutes. I had timed it perfectly. I maintained low level and started back, flying one klick east of the last route. From experience, I knew there would not be time for the enemy to set up an ambush. General Cushman and his party anticipated our arrival and were on board within five seconds after the skids touched down. With a "clear" from the door gunners, we headed southwest about one klick and turned back west, paralleling the DMZ and always maintaining low level. I flew a winding course that was lower than the tops of the sand dunes. I turned back north, and, within a minute, picked up the location of Charlie 1.

I made a quick call when we were two minutes from the LZ to make sure there would not be smoke. Everything went well. They knew the routine. After picking up General Cushman and low leveling back to Dong Ha, we gained fifteen hundred feet of altitude and in ten minutes, arrived at Quang Tri. One of the general's aides, a full colonel, tapped me on the right shoulder and yelled over the noise, "Outstanding job, Lieutenant."

He extended his arm and gave us a meaningful thumbs-up, which made this army helicopter pilot and his crew proud. Even though General Cushman did not see us salute him, we did so with respect. Over the intercom, I said, "All right, back to the real war. We can tell our grandkids we met a three-star general today."

My fourth VIP mission was to fly Vietnamese Premier Nguyen Cao Ky to three outposts located along the DMZ. They were designated Charlie 2, Alpha 1, and Alpha 2. These were ARVN artillery firebases. Also on the flight were three ARVN generals, including General Lam and General Truong, as well as Colonel Kelley.

Ky was tall and slender. He wore a freshly starched tailored black flight suit with a scarlet ascot. A former fighter pilot, he had gained notoriety for his flamboyant manner. He was no stranger to this area but had seen only it from high altitude. I flew the mission as we always flew north of Dong Ha. The rice en route was two feet high this time of year. I made sure our skids were in the growing rice, flying at more than one hundred knots. I rose only to go over the three-foot dikes. We then flew around the sand dunes and bomb craters to the three outposts, maintaining only two to four feet off the ground. I must admit I flew lower and was much more abrupt with the controls than when I flew General Cushman. Since Ky was an aviator, I was hoping he would have no trouble with low-level flying.

The entire mission took more than two and a half hours because they spent time at each outpost. Finally I took him back to the parade field at Hue. I was firmly on the ground when my crew chief spoke over the intercom, sounding worried. "Lieutenant, Ky really wants to talk to you."

This can't be good, I thought.

I told my crew chief to tell him we had an emergency. We had to go. No sooner had I said that than Premier Ky tapped me on the shoulder and motioned for me to take off my flight helmet. I noticed Colonel Kelley was on the ground right outside the cockpit staring at me. Now I knew I was going to hear something like, "What was that kind of flying all about?"

I raised up my tinted visor and took off my flight helmet. Over the noise, I yelled a questioning, "Yes, sir?"

From two feet away Ky yelled back, "Number one American cowboy!"

We shook hands and I thanked him. I took it as a compliment. With a smile, I put my helmet back on and glanced at Colonel Kelley, who was still staring at me. If I could have read his mind, I'm sure he was thinking, *You can't fool me. You were probably showing off.* But he never mentioned it.

-12-

CHRISTMAS WITH BOB AND RAQUEL

We are about 30 minute flight time from the DMZ. I live in the MACV Compound, so we are pretty safe. There are about 200 of us. The only trouble is that the VC like to mortar us regularly. I'm getting good at scrambling out of bed, grabbing my flak vest, helmet, and M-16. By the time the second round hits, I'm in a perimeter bunker. You asked what I would like for Christmas. The only thing I could possibly need would be some foot powder, toothpaste and toothbrush. I just thought of something else. How about some canned fruit, no apricots.

——————— 02 DEC 67 Letter to Dad and Bill

If something funny didn't happen every hour, we were inclined to create it. One way we entertained ourselves was to fill a few empty M60 ammo canisters with sand to make "bombs" to drop on targets.

Sampans are small flat-bottom skiffs made of grass reeds. If we spotted an empty one in a canal or river, we maintained one thousand feet flying at about fifty knots, and I slowly went through bombing instructions to the two door gunners. I tried to imitate the pilots who flew the B-29 Superfortresses in the World War II movies I had seen as a kid.

"Pilot to bombardier, pilot to bombardier. Target in sight," I would say over the intercom. "Open bomb bay door. Prepare to drop. Prepare to drop."

As we flew over our objective, they would throw out the ammo cans, which weighed about fifteen pounds, saying, "Bombs away."

We would try to hit the sampan and sink it. It made for a lot of laughs in the aircraft. We decided that those B-29 bomber crews were a lot better than we were. We never got close to hitting a thing, but we saw some big splashes.

On several occasions, I received radio calls between missions from Da Nang pilots who were in our AO. I told them to come up on our UHF general-conversation frequency. After a brief update, they usually asked me who was flying in the right seat. I told them Warrant Officer Rickenbacker, referring to my childhood hero, Eddie Rickenbacker—a World War I ace and the first aviator to be awarded the Medal of Honor.

"Who's he?" they would question. "Say again."

I would come back, "Rickenbacker. He's a new guy, can't read a map too good, but my gosh, he can fly." With that, I terminated the conversation, smiled at my copilot, and thought how the Da Nang crew would get back to HQ trying to figure out who Rickenbacker was.

★★★★

Two days before Christmas, I pulled rank on the men. We found out that Bob Hope was coming to Da Nang for his annual Christmas visit, and the incredibly beautiful Raquel Welch was going to be with him. The chance to see an American legend like Bob Hope—in the eyes of soldiers, probably the most popular guy in the history of American entertainment—was pretty exciting. He always brought the sweetest, nicest, funniest, and most attractive ladies with him. Raquel Welch was tops in every one of those categories, admired and desired by all. This was literally the chance of a lifetime.

Right after the nightly briefing, I said to my men, "You guys know I have never pulled rank on you." Then I talked in detail about Bob Hope's visit on Christmas Day, emphasizing that Raquel Welch would be present. "I am pulling rank for the first time on this one."

I waited a few moments for it to soak in, and then I looked at each one of them. I had the feeling McKinsey knew what I was going to say because of his slight grin.

"I'm staying and the rest of you are going. However, I need one volunteer to stay with me and fly any missions that may come up while you're gone."

Almost in unison, they all quietly said, "Hey, Boss, I'll stay."

"OK, since Pullen is the old married guy at twenty-six, you can stay with me. Seeing Raquel might be bad for your heart."

In the middle of the laughter, Toews spoke up, "It's only right that Tom and the boss stay since they saw Bob Hope during World War II."

That cracked everybody up.

Tom and I had a memorable Christmas Day. Just knowing that all the men were getting to see Bob Hope and Raquel Welch made us feel good, and we talked about it all day. We started Christmas Day by taking hot turkey, dressing, and gravy in mermite containers to five outposts on the DMZ. We did not open one container. In the Christmas spirit, we ate cold C-ration turkey loaf. The troops always came first with us. I changed my call sign that day to Santa Claus 2-1. At one outpost, we heard Christmas carols playing in the background when I called at two minutes inbound.

"Did you guys hear that?" I asked over the intercom.

They confirmed with a joyful, "Yes!" It gave me a quick, nostalgic chill.

Later we took two Catholic priests, one American and one Vietnamese, to an orphanage. We shut down while the two priests walked among the kids for an hour. We gave the kids our remaining C-rations before we left.

We returned to Hue and picked up a package that had been sent to me from the high school student council of my hometown, Shawnee, Oklahoma. They had sent two hundred five-piece packages of assorted Wrigley's gum. We had one thousand wrapped sticks of gum.

"Tom, I have the best idea," I said. "Let's hover down the main street of Hue and toss some out."

We started at the north end of the Perfume River Bridge and flew east. We passed slowly over the street that paralleled the Perfume River, flying about one hundred feet. We saw no one.

"Dang, this was a complete bust," I said. "Go ahead and throw some out anyway."

Tom said, "Well, Boss, at least we tried."

I started to turn left to go back to the airfield when our crew chief, Heidi "Bud" Atanian, shouted over the intercom, "My God, look at that. Turn around."

We completed a 180. There, right in front of us, were hundreds of kids in the market square.

Atanian and our door gunner started throwing out the rest of the gum. What a sight it was—one thousand sticks of silver-wrapped gum floating down to all those kids, their hands reaching skyward.

Flying back to the airfield, we joyfully chattered about the experience. After we landed and while we cooled the turbine engine at flight idle to prepare for shutdown, Atanian said, "I have another idea. Let's tie red and green smoke grenades to both skids, pull the pins, and fly over the compound."

We smiled and laughed like kids.

"Way to go," I said. "This will be great." I called compound headquarters and told them to watch. Using WD-1 communication wire to attach the smoke grenades, we were soon ready to go. We pulled the pins thirty seconds out and headed over the compound at twenty knots. We knew it was a beautiful sight from the ground. The smoke grenades were still going when we did a 180 and came back over. One of the grenades came loose, dropped in the compound, and filled it with green smoke. It was an accident, but everyone thought we did it on purpose. We all ended up laughing, and, to this day, Tom, Atanian, and I recall that Christmas as our most memorable.

Everyone who went to see Bob Hope and Raquel Welch came back with nonstop stories that lasted a week. Told with excitement, they were as vivid as being there. I could almost smell Raquel's perfume.

–13–

NEW YEAR—ANOTHER DAY

Almost every day the ARVN fly their H-34s to Hue—all dressed in freshly pressed flight suits with colored ascots to go into town all day. Meanwhile we fly all their resupply and medevac missions. ARVN operations know we'll take any mission. They point to a spot on our map, give us a frequency, and what color smoke will be popped. The frequency is seldom right. When they do answer, you can't understand them, and it's never the right smoke. We always go in anyway, usually hot. . . . We like this kind of stuff.

30 DEC 67 Letter to Diane

The last day of the year was on its way out. Weather for the last two weeks had been a constant drizzle that produced visibility no better than a quarter or half-mile, so each mission had to be flown low level. Even slowing to eighty knots, the terrain under you moves by quite fast when you're so low. New Year's Eve was brought up a few times during our nightly briefing but with little enthusiasm. A New Year's Eve party was even talked about. We decided we might make plans later.

Before the first flight of the day, the crew chief pulled a preflight inspection. This could take as much as thirty minutes, even though he had conducted a postflight inspection after the last mission the previous day. During this time, the door gunners readied both M60s. Their job also included assuring us that there was plenty of ammunition,

C-rations, and water. We usually carried six to ten canisters of ammo for each M60 with two hundred rounds in each canister. Both pilots conducted a preflight that took much less time.

Each crew chief inspected in detail the intricate workings of that incredible flying machine, the UH-1 Huey. They took their jobs seriously. It was good to accompany the crew chief during his inspection once a week and have him demonstrate his expertise. At some point during his inspection, I would say, "I didn't know that." That statement made the crew chief feel a notch higher in importance—and he was. Each one did his job with dedication. They all were also outstanding door gunners.

Since it was the end of the month, the crew chief, Dee Truscott, the gunner, Bob Brown, my right seat pilot, Dick Messer, and I decided to go to Da Nang and pick up the monthly pay. This was my first time back to company headquarters since mid-September. I had avoided going back because of the endless questions I anticipated having to answer: How are you guys getting so much flight time? Why are you taking so many hits? What's it like reporting to Colonel Kelley? Why is it that we only talk to the junior pilot when you call on the landline? How are you pulling so many medevacs? How did you put yourselves in position to get so many KIAs? Are you ever going across the border? Why do you fly all your approaches to LZs so steep and fast? Are you low leveling when you should be flying at altitude?

Major Ward never asked these questions. I'm sure he'd been checking on me regularly. If we met on the tarmac, he would return my salute and give me a quick nod, then smile as if to say, "Good job." I found out years later that Major Ward and Colonel Kelley were both proud of each of us. They said that they had never seen a small autonomous unit perform so well. However, the operations officer, the executive officer, my platoon leader, the company standardization instructor pilot, and other pilots constantly tried to corner me. The only thing I liked about Da Nang was the hot showers.

Even though the weather remained bad, low leveling throughout our area of operation and certainly to Da Nang along the coast was easy. I picked up the pay after signing for it and was approached by our operations officer who told me about some passengers who needed to get back north ASAP. An army major with MACV, a chaplain, a marine lance corporal, and a gunnery sergeant had been assigned to Quang Tri and were on their way north. Quang Tri was their first assignment in country. You could see the "new-guy" look in their faces along with their clean, not-yet-faded uniforms. I liked to talk with new guys to assure them that they were joining a good unit. No matter where they were headed, I told them the unit was the best outfit in I Corps. But after all the kind words, the pilots at Hue made sure any new guy remembered his first helicopter ride with a Black Cat. We took them flying our kind of low level—never getting more than three feet off the ground—hit the top of the first tree in sight, and jerked them around with each maneuver. It was no different from how we flew in and out of hot LZs, but no new guy was ready for it.

On this particular flight, Private Brown decided to put even more anxiety into our group of passengers. Before we lit the fire in the turbine, Brownie walked close by the passengers sitting in the cargo section and acted like an airline terminal announcer.

"Good morning, ladies and gentlemen, and welcome aboard," he began. "The pilots have just informed me that visibility is less than a quarter mile with heavy turbulence. We will fly directly to Quang Tri—that is, if we are not shot down. For your personal comfort, the pilots have chosen to fly at an altitude of two feet. After takeoff, keep your seat belt on and your head down. Now, all you new guys who want on get on."

By now, we were all laughing inside but acted as if this was a normal announcement.

We went through an abbreviated start-up procedure, hovered out to Marble Mountain's active runway, got clearance, and low leveled north. As we went under Da Nang's main runway flight path for high-performance aircraft, we spotted a few people lining China Beach. Each one had to lie flat or scramble out of the way as we proceeded north around the northern point of Da Nang Bay and Hai Van Pass. About ten minutes later, I decided to start inland at an angle to stay south of Hue and locate Highway 1. We could then follow the road all the way to Quang Tri. Our gunners were getting ready for any situation and shot several bursts through their M60s to make sure the weapons were functioning OK, making our passengers even jumpier.

When we left the coast and started inland, we were sure no other aircraft would be in the area due to the weather. I had Messer switch to Hue operations to report our location. Without the squelch on, we couldn't hear them. The squelch is a circuit that suppresses the output of a radio receiver if the signal strength falls below a certain level. We used it only when necessary due to the constant loud static when not broadcasting. With the squelch on, we were able to receive the troops' weak radio broadcast. Faintly we could hear them yell to contact Water Dog Alpha on fox mike code Amber. Obviously there was an emergency. Messer looked Amber up in the SOI and put me up channel one. I responded, "Water Dog Alpha, this is Black Cat 2-1, over."

Faintly we heard, "Black Cat, this is Water Dog Alpha. We need medevac, over."

"Roger that, Alpha. What is your location?"

Not wanting to delay the medevac, he gave me his coordinates straight out, not in shackles. Messer, who was a solid pilot, had been in country more than seven months and was close to making AC. He found the location quickly on his map. Phu Bai was in line to the medevac location. I thought it was best to drop off our passengers in case we got into a firefight or needed the room for wounded.

Messer contacted Phu Bai and told them that we would be leaving four passengers on the east end of their active. They rogered and acknowledged that there had been no traffic all day due to the poor weather. I think we woke up the tower operator.

We dropped the passengers with their gear. Truscott had told them we had an emergency and to stay in the area. We were on the ground no more than fifteen seconds.

We immediately contacted Water Dog Alpha, reporting we were zero five from their location.

Water Dog Alpha came back, "Black Cat 2-1, we are taking fire from our east, hardly any visibility. Are you sure you can find us?"

"Roger, Alpha, we are on our way," I said. "Give me a long count, and, when you hear us getting close, pop smoke."

There was a too-long delay, so I came back, "Uh, Alpha, do you copy?"

"This is Alpha. What's a long count, over?"

Few ground troops knew we had FM homing capability, which could be used in this situation. As long as someone was actually broadcasting on an FM frequency that we had tuned in, the FM homing course indicator told us with a needle in the localizer if we were left or right of the position transmitting. It's not a precision instrument, but with experience, it works good enough to get us within two hundred meters of a position. As long as someone was broadcasting, we could follow the signal. We considered a long count to ten and a short count to five and used one or the other, depending on how far we thought we were from the troops we were trying to find.

I quickly transmitted, "Alpha, count to ten. Slow."

It would have been almost impossible to locate these guys in this weather without the aid of the FM homing device. Without it, we would also have been exposed to the enemy too long trying to locate them. Alpha began his long count, and I corrected my route accordingly when I cross-checked the indicator needle about every five seconds. Brown opened up with three short bursts from his M60. I had no time to ask. Must have been at an enemy target.

Two minutes later came, "2-1, we hear you. Popping smoke."

We strained to confirm smoke, but had no sighting. I knew we could be in trouble if we flew by their position. With poor visibility we had to be right on them. We were going ninety knots at ten feet.

Then thirty seconds later, the radio cracked, "We hear you. You're close." This was followed by, "You just went by. Can't see you."

At that moment, the indicator needle swung full to the right, then in two seconds centered because we had passed them and were now moving straight away from them. With no visual contact, we had to turn back left to find them. I was sure glad that my constant crosscheck of the instrument had tracked the passage so I knew to turn left. I heard the loud cracking of automatic small arms fire. We had to be close. Both of our gunners opened up.

"Making a one-eighty. Give me a short count."

I made a hard banking left turn and lined up the needle once again while the radio operator began his count to five.

"Black Cat, we hear you. Popping smoke."

This time I nailed it. We went right over the LZ before I had a chance to call the color of the smoke. I bottomed the collective and pulled back on the cyclic to slow my ground speed without gaining altitude. When our ground speed became slow enough, I kicked in the left pedal to slow faster by going against the torque of the main rotor. I came back and landed.

Immediately an American captain and two ARVN soldiers were loaded on our Huey.

"All on board. Clear left," Truscott said.

Brown gave two clicks on the intercom. I glanced back, and the captain gave me a look that said, "I can't believe you made it."

I checked again with Alpha for the location of their last-known enemy fire and low leveled out in the opposite direction. Another voice came on the radio, probably the ranking non-commissioned officer (NCO). "2-1, glad you found us. You all did a good job, thanks."

I gave him two clicks to indicate that I had received his transmission. His comment made everything worthwhile. We were still up Phu Bai ADF, and I changed direction toward the facility. I pulled in all the power the aircraft would take and flew direct to the medevac pad. En route, Truscott and Brown opened up several times with their M60s. Messer had Phu Bai tower notify the medical facility and confirmed there was no traffic. He asked to have stretchers standing by.

After unloading our wounded, I turned the controls over to Dick and then spoke to the gunners. "Hey Truscott, Brownie, you guys get any back there?"

"Not sure," Truscott replied, "but I put my fire right on a lot of muzzle flashes."

Brown came on the intercom. "Got one for sure, only ten feet away, and think I got four or five more."

"Good job," I said. "Let's go find our passengers."

"Say, Boss, think our passengers are where we left them?" Dick asked.

With a laugh as I lit an old C-ration Pall Mall, I said, "I bet if we hover down the runway, they'll find us."

We weren't on the runway fifteen seconds when all four men came strolling along with their gear in both hands to intersect our path.

"Hey, Dick," I said. "Play like we don't see them and keep going past them."

Truscott started laughing while we went fifty meters past the new guys. "Lieutenant, these guys are going nuts!"

We hovered back, and they scrambled on board while unknown to them we all were still laughing over the intercom.

The weather stayed lousy the rest of the day. We called it "WOXOF," a humorous term from flight school that means Weather Obscure Zero Visibility With Fog. The flight to Quang Tri and back to Hue was routine, though the visibility stayed below a half-mile. Dick flew a comfortable ninety-knot five to fifteen feet off the deck while I got on the radio and cleared us of any outgoing artillery along Highway 1. I made contact with Hue operations to give our location and see if there were any missions. I choked down one more five-year-old C-ration cigarette, this time, a Winston. Those things tasted terrible by the end of the day. That's one reason I quit smoking the day I left Vietnam.

Back in the compound, I got together with all the pilots for a briefing. With a smile, we told them we had forgotten the shrimp, steaks, beer, and champagne for the New Year's Eve party. I had the next day's missions handed to me by a new operations officer, a major assigned to coordinate missions and generally keep up with us. He was already the third one since September. None of them enjoyed this duty since I never informed them where we were or what we were doing. Things were always changing, and we just did not have the time.

Whenever one of the majors cornered me and wanted to know the details of any one mission, I waited for him to quit talking and then calmly asked if he was qualified with an M60. They always answered with a very weak, "Why yes, why?"

"Are you sure, sir?" I said. "Because the best way to find out about any of our missions is to go with us and man one of the machine guns as a door gunner all day and possibly into the night. If you go, we'll depend on you to fire that M60 in any situation. We take off at 0600."

They never accepted.

Soon after, during one of Colonel Kelley's briefings, he was chewing out everyone when he abruptly pointed to me and said, "These guys are the only ones that know what they're doing." That was the end of any operations officer.

As we broke up our meeting that night, I asked, "Anybody want to go on a two- or three-day in-country R&R? Any of you guys want to check out the Saigon warriors or lie on the beach at Cam Rahn Bay?"

"We'll think about it," came the common reply. None of us ever went.

"Hey, one more thing. You guys know it's New Year's Eve?"

"Who gives a rat's butt?" Toews said.

"Al said what I was going to say," Dedrick said.

Mac smiled. "One day closer to DEROS."

"Yeah, I agree," I chimed in. "Negative New Year's party. Mac, when do you go home?"

"Nine February."

"Mac," I said, "you're getting short. You give the word when you want to finis fly, and I'll send you to Da Nang to hang up your chicken plate and helmet. Then you can sit around and soak up some rays and read a book. You sure deserve it. And write your mom a letter."

"OK, Boss," he said with his slight smile.

I didn't tell McKinsey that the Red Cross had contacted me through HQ because he had not written home in four months. It was so hard for those back home to understand what it was like to fly combat. They didn't want to know. I wrote only eleven letters to my parents and five of those were in the first two months of my tour.

I went to my hootch and started a letter to Diane. I was tired from flying five-and-a-half hours low level in this weather. It was 10:30. After taking the usual thirty-second forty-five-degree well water shower, I was soon asleep. I woke when a few troops shot tracers into the air at midnight. Immediately afterward, our early warning radar system for incoming rockets or mortars was set off, and the siren sent everyone scrambling to their bunkers. We were taking up a firing position with our M16s when Tom and Skulborstad came in and sheepishly told me it was their homemade New Year's fireworks mortar round that set off the siren. They called it "a lousy Roman candle."

"Let's go get some sleep, little boys," I said and headed back to my bunk. I was proud that it was my guys who had pulled the stunt. All clear was sounded two hours later. I slept all right. January 1, 1968, was going to be just another day.

—14—

21 JAN 68

The small picture you sent me I have taped inside my SOI. I use it about 50 times a day. When I tell my pilot to look up a frequency while flying, he always says, "Boy, Lieutenant, you sure have a pretty wife."

07 JAN 68 Letter to Diane

The new year brought daily briefings of escalating enemy activity. The North Vietnamese were making a strong presence in I Corps with well-equipped soldiers, and everywhere we flew, we encountered more groundfire. The latest rumor was that an attack at Khe Sanh, seventy miles northwest of Hue, was imminent. All of the outposts around Khe Sanh had been under intense enemy pressure.

Since McKinsey was only three weeks from his DEROS date, I sent him to Da Nang on January 18. I made him promise to quit flying, get in the sun, read a couple of books, and tape-record an album of the Mamas & the Papas for me. I knew we were going to miss him but was sure glad he was going home. We had become good friends.

On the ship that came to pick up Mac was his replacement, W-1 Richard Gilmore. He was quiet and ready to learn. I was sure he would fit in perfectly.

During my briefing the night of January 20 in Colonel Kelley's office, he indicated that conditions were getting more intense. It was rare for Colonel Kelley to request a one-on-one briefing with me. He told me it was urgent that both of our ships report to the senior MACV advisor at Quang Tri, the next morning.

Tom Pullen, who had just received his AC orders, would be flying with the newest pilot, Gilmore, in Crew Chief Seghetti's ship. Pullen could have been an AC forty-five days earlier, if there had been an opening. I didn't mind the delay because I liked flying with him. He was an unflappable, skilled, good-natured pilot. His call sign became Black Cat 2-7.

Pullen took off fifteen minutes before us because my aircraft had a mechanical problem. While our crew chief, Thomason, made our repairs, Dedrick asked if he could fly with me. I always welcomed an AC in the right seat, so I said sure. It was pretty rare for two ACs to fly together.

When Dedrick and I landed at La Vang to pick up supplies, Pullen was already on his way to Huong Hoa. Pullen and I had monitored several radio transmissions from Lieutenant Colonel Smith saying Huong Hoa was under artillery fire and probing ground attacks for the last eight hours. Lieutenant Colonel Smith wanted to get as much ammo and medical supplies to them as possible in case of a full-scale ground attack, which appeared imminent, so we quickly loaded the vital supplies.

As we headed for Huong Hoa, Pullen radioed, "Black Cat 2-1, this is 2-7, come up uniform."

I could tell from Tom's voice that there was a problem. We both came up on our predesignated frequency. "2-7, what's up?" I asked.

"The ground fire is more than we have ever seen, Boss. Seghetti got shot through the foot. We had to abort. On our way back to Quang Tri hospital."

"OK, take care of Seghetti. We will attempt to get in," I said, adding, "I'm switching to Huong Hoa frequency at this time. Out."

Over the intercom, I told the gunners to clear their weapons and then said, "Dedrick, what do you think?"

He glanced over. "I think we are going to earn our combat pay."

I depressed the transmit trigger. "Alpha Lima, this is Black Cat 2-1. We are 04 from your position. Is your LZ clear?"

I had to ask because when outposts are under attack, LZs can contain all kinds of debris including concertina wire, a kind of coiled razor wire.

"LZ clear," Lima said.

At two minutes from the LZ, I dropped the collective and started falling out of the sky. We were about one klick away, and already we could pick up muzzle flashes. Our gunners returned fire. There were plenty of targets. I concentrated on closing speed, trying to get out of the sky as fast as possible when a silly thought came to me—it was hard to believe so many people were mad at us.

Within four hundred meters of the LZ, the automatic weapons sounded like popcorn popping right in my ear. It took all the aircraft's power to stop in the small LZ. The low RPM audio sounded right when our skids softly touched the ground. I told the gunners to unload everything and put a fresh box of ammo into their machine guns. As Dedrick looked back at the supplies being unloaded, I checked the instrument panel for normal readings.

"Clear," Dedrick said when everything was unloaded.

The ship was much lighter now. I pulled in all the power, and the Huey sprung from the LZ. We stayed right on the deck. By staying low level, we were not such an easy target. Our machine guns started firing immediately, and after four minutes, we climbed to two thousand feet and headed toward La Vang.

"Lima, this is 2-1. I'll be back in about one hour with more supplies," I called.

"2-1, we are taking so much fire. I don't know if we can get to the supplies you left."

"Roger, I'll report on my way back."

The guys on the ground, like our crew chiefs, always figured things out. We switched frequencies and contacted Pullen on UHF. I knew Tom would be waiting for an update, and I wanted one too.

"Tom, how is Seghetti?"

"He's OK, just mad he got shot," Tom said.

"I am 05 from La Vang to pick up more supplies and go back. I will need you if we get into trouble."

"What about a gunner?" Tom would be short one with Seghetti injured.

"Get a marine," I said. "We have never seen one yet that didn't like to fight."

We loaded up and headed back. I reported to Lima when we were five minutes out.

"We got the supplies," Lima told us. "The LZ is clear. Will cover you on your way in."

From altitude, we could see the outpost five klicks away. I decided to come in low level and from a different direction than we had come the first time. We dropped down and covered the last three klicks close to the ground. We heard an enormous amount of enemy fire and saw muzzle flashes throughout the approach. The NVA had been preparing for our return.

I navigated perfectly to the LZ, only having it in sight the last three hundred to four hundred meters. I knew Lima could not have seen our approach, so I reported inbound at one minute. The outpost was laying out a barrage of fire at all suspected enemy locations to protect us from taking hits and failing to deliver the much needed supplies.

Once again, the landing was like a controlled crash without damage. The door gunners threw out the ammo and supplies then reloaded immediately. I pulled the transmit trigger on the cyclic and said, "Lima, we're clear." I wanted to inform Lima that we were on our way out. I planned a different exit.

I pulled full power and low leveled out. I had begun to dive into a ravine when Lima transmitted, "2-1, you can't believe what is coming up at you."

I acknowledged with two clicks. We had our hands full.

We made a cyclic climb over the ground-level foundation of an abandoned 1950s French fort. The area about the size of two football fields was relatively flat and covered with copper-colored dirt. We cleared the crest before diving down the other side, never flying higher than five feet off the ground.

We drew heavy enemy fire well over two klicks from the LZ. When the firing stopped, we climbed to altitude. My two door gunners, Brown and Crew Chief Thomason, were calm and precise. They had saved us from being shot down.

I radioed Tom, and he told me about a plan for a combat assault to relieve Huong Hoa. There were aircraft coming from Da Nang to execute the CA. Dedrick and I thought the CA could be successful, if the LZ was properly prepared.

When we landed at La Vang, I motioned to Tom to go with me to talk to Lieutenant Colonel Smith. I wanted him to delay the CA until an artillery barrage or two flights of F4s prepared any LZ. I was sure my Cat Killer buddies could get at least four high-performance aircraft to drop napalm and fire an enormous amount of ordnance to prepare the LZ. Since Tom and I had just been out there, we knew the strength of the enemy, and I thought we would carry weight in the decision-making process. I was wrong.

Captain Steiner, our 282nd operations officer, intercepted us and asked how things were.

"It was the worst we've ever seen, sir," I told him. "Where are you going to land the ships?"

"At the old French fort."

"Sir, we were just there. We flew low level right over it. The whole place was surrounded and in control of the enemy," I said.

Captain Steiner sought out our new company commander, Major Rice (not his real name), who had replaced Major Chuck Ward when he DEROSed the previous month. They said to come with them to talk with Lieutenant Colonel Smith.

I briefly explained the situation to Smith and told him it would be impossible to land seven ships without at least a one-hour artillery barrage or two flights of jets preparing the LZ. Then I suggested an alternative to the CA. I proposed that Tom and I go back to Huong Hoa as a single ship with troops seven times with an Alley Cat gunship escort. I told him I had already made it in twice that day without gunships.

I thought my solution to Huong Hoa's predicament made sense. I clearly and forcefully repeated that there was no way we could land this many aircraft in formation without terrible results and that our three Alley Cat gunships were not enough to cover all of them. No one else said a word.

When I had finished, Lieutenant Colonel Smith said, "We are going to go and go now."

My judgment had never been questioned since I had become AC. If Major Ward had still been in command, I knew he would have

140

backed me up. I pressed Smith to reconsider, but he had made up his mind.

I was upset, and apparently it showed. Smith pointed at me and raised his voice. "Lieutenant, you are getting out of line. Do you understand?"

He wanted this CA to happen, and he was going to be in the lead ship. Tom and I walked back to our aircraft.

Fighting to hold in my frustration, I asked Tom if he had found a door gunner.

"Yes, a marine on security detail volunteered," he told me.

When we got to his aircraft, the marine was already behind the machine gun and looked ready, but the M60 trigger mechanism on a D model Huey is located on two handles in the back of the weapon, and I had to be sure he was familiar with it.

"Tom, make sure that marine knows how to fire that thing."

"Yeah, Boss, we checked him out," Tom said.

Three Alley Cat gunships and the aircraft from Da Nang started up. As the aircraft started up, the troops loaded. The soldiers were all RF/PF Vietnamese reserves and local militia. Tom had formed up and was number seven in the CA. The lead aircraft transmitted over the designated tactical frequency, "All aircraft report when ready."

I got the worst feeling in my gut when I heard that voice. It was McKinsey.

Within seconds, I transmitted, "Mac, is that you? Go uniform. What are you doing here?"

I was furious. He had only about two weeks before going home. Then came Mac's answer, "They didn't have enough pilots, so I volunteered."

"OK, Mac." I drew a deep, steadying breath. "It's really bad out there. I hope the Alley Cats do the job."

There weren't enough soldiers for all of the aircraft, so it left mine empty since I had just returned from our mission and was the last to arrive. We made a decision to load more ammo because we were sure the troops would need it. This put me fifteen minutes behind the other seven ships and the three Alley Cat gunships. The plan was for the Alley Cats to prepare the LZ (the old French fort) and for the seven ships to land immediately behind them and unload the ARVN troops. Lieutenant Colonel Smith would then lead them to relieve the Houng Hoa outpost.

With McKinsey and Steiner in the lead, the seven aircraft flew in a close, staggered trail formation so as to set down at the fort together, maintaining the formation. All the ACs in the CA had heard about my resupply missions to Houng Hoa. I had reported flying over the old fort during our second exit route after resupplying the outpost. However, the pilots and gunships were never warned about the severity of the enemy situation that I had reported. So now everyone was ready for a typical simple combat assault that appeared no different from any other—but it was. The NVA suspected there would be more attempts to resupply and had sufficient time to move closer to Houng Hoa and reinforce the only other possible landing zone—the old French fort.

There had been no preparation of the LZ from fighter aircraft or artillery before the ships arrived. The gunships had time for only one run and reported enemy movement in a tree line. As soon as our Hueys began to land at the old French fort, the enemy opened up with enormous gunfire at close range. The trap was sprung, and the well-armed enemy engulfed the LZ. Our gunships continued to support the landing until they had expended all their ammunition.

As we approached the fort, we could see Hueys on the CA coming back. Major Rice radioed us that the enemy had completely overrun the location. All the aircraft had exited. He told us that the lead aircraft was brought down by a rocket-propelled grenade (RPG). That was McKinsey's ship.

I heard later that as soon as McKinsey and Steiner landed, they came under heavy automatic fire. As the RF/PF troops unloaded, the enemy instantly engaged them. When McKinsey and Steiner exited the LZ, they were hit broadside with an RPG. Their aircraft burst into flames and crashed. Two rescue ships made several passes over the burning Huey, but no survivors were seen.

Major Rice gave us an order to go back to Quang Tri. For five minutes, Dedrick and I talked over the intercom. We asked ourselves: What if we threw out all of our ammo, landed at the French fort, and looked for survivors? We both agreed the chances were zero that we could make it.

That evening, back at Hue, I still wasn't sure of our decision. The thought of losing Mac seemed impossible. Several times Pullen, Messer, and Aye retold how McKinsey's ship had burst into a ball of flames. They said that even the main rotor blades were on fire. They saw no survivors. We got a report that all of the delivered RF/PF troops died in the LZ.

In all of the emotional chaos after the CA, Tom and I remembered the marine who had volunteered to fly as Tom's door gunner. He was wounded twice but had killed several enemy soldiers within ten feet of the aircraft. When he was carried on the stretcher from the helicopter, he asked if we needed him anymore that day. That brave eighteen-year-old lance corporal survived.

Years later, he contacted me wanting to know if he had done his duty that day. "You sure did, Marine," I told him, even though he was then a doctor in Lawton, Oklahoma—Dr. Rick Brittingham.

At 4:00 a.m. the next day, January 22, I was awakened and told there were two survivors who had made it back to Khe Sanh. A thought went instantly through my head: *It just has to be McKinsey.* I carefully woke Pullen. I wanted him with me.

The thirty-minute flight to Khe Sanh seemed to last forever. As we approached Khe Sanh under darkness, mortars were hitting the facility. I flew directly to what appeared to be the command bunker. Over the intercom, I told Tom to stay in the ship while I went to find the survivors. I told him to keep the aircraft at full RPM. I put my flight helmet on the hook above my head in the cockpit, and Thomason opened my door and slid back my armored side plate. I headed out into the dimly lit bunker complex.

I asked everyone I saw if they knew of any army pilots, but there were no coherent responses. Several times, I raised my voice and asked, "Are there any army pilots in here?"

I went from bunker to bunker following the deep trenches that connected them. The bunkers were about fifteen meters apart, and I could hear the constant impact of mortar rounds. I hoped none had hit our aircraft.

Tom followed me by hovering the distance as I continued my search. As I entered the fourth bunker, I literally came face to face with Captain Steiner. He had heard our Huey and come out to investigate. He was obviously fatigued and had dried blood on his neck and right sleeve. Stooped over behind him was one of our men from Da Nang. Steiner said his name was Williams, a door gunner. I did not know Williams.

He was in a lot of pain, so I supported him by lifting him under his left armpit to help him onto our aircraft. While covering the short distance, I heard him repeat over and over, "My God, the pain!" From the waist down, his back was covered with dry, caked blood. He lay bent over on our cargo floor.

I started to go around to get in the cockpit when Steiner forcibly grabbed me and yelled over all the noise, "Are you sure this thing will fly?"

I knew that had to be a stress-induced question. I yelled, "Yes, sir, this is a good ship. We need to get you out of here."

Steiner said, "We must get Williams more medical attention."

Mortars continued to impact the south end of the runway as we took off and headed north. In the smoke, the beautiful little waterfall east of Khe Sanh looked dreary. We climbed to altitude.

After Captain Steiner put on my door gunner's helmet, I asked, "What happened to Mac? Is McKinsey alive?" My breath seemed to catch in my throat as I waited for his answer.

"Negative," Steiner said. "He's dead."

I knew better than to question this fine officer, but I couldn't help but ask him again, "Are you sure?"

Steiner said that after the crash, the survivors exited the Huey through the windshield. McKinsey began shooting the NVA soldiers as they came up the hill after them. Steiner's voice was slow and weary as he told me the story: "I was trying to get Lieutenant Colonel Smith free from the burning aircraft. Smith was dead. Grenades started coming in, so Williams and I went to get Mac and get out of there. As I approached him, he slumped over, head first. I grabbed him to get up and run. There was a bullet hole in the back of his flight helmet. I raised the helmet up and there was nothing. Nothing but red pulp. Completely gone."

After a moment, Steiner continued. "McKinsey could have gotten on two rescue ships that came in to help us. Those ships took so many hits they had to leave while I was trying to free Smith from the burning helicopter. One ship was no more than ten feet away from Mac. He stayed to protect me. Since the bullet had come from behind, we knew we were being surrounded. Williams, an ARVN soldier, and I crawled for an hour toward Khe Sanh. The NVA chased us all night. They had dogs. We got to Khe Sanh. We came too close to their perimeter, and the marines opened up on us with an M79 grenade launcher. That's how Williams got wounded. He took most of the impact. I started yelling, and eventually they let us in."

Tom and I took Steiner and Williams back to Da Nang. We landed in front of the operations hootch with the entire 282nd personnel there to welcome them.

We didn't say much about that day. It never should have happened. A lieutenant has little chance to influence events when a high-ranking officer perceives that any advice from a young aviator will make him look unprofessional and an indecisive leader.

One door gunner, Jerry Elliot, jumped off a rescue ship that day to help and has not been accounted for to this day.

We couldn't believe McKinsey was gone. He was the best. I did not allow myself to dwell on his memory that day due to nonstop obligations, and when I returned home, adjusting to the real world occupied my mind—yet I still thought of Mac every day of my tour and have every day since.

I located Mac's mom and dad and wrote them a letter in August 1986. Part of it read: "I often sought out Mac to get his opinion about other pilots, aircraft, gunners, and crew chiefs. Really though, I just liked his company and felt we were much alike. He is the only pilot I asked about his future plans and requested he go by my folks' home in Shawnee, Oklahoma, to say hello on his way to his stateside assignment."

I concluded the letter by writing, "Your son was the very best America can offer. It was your influence that made him the person he was. He was loved by all those who knew him and will never be forgotten. When I go to the wall—when I think I can—I want to touch his name and say, 'Mac, we miss you.' Sincerely yours, Bob."

I went to the Vietnam Wall in Washington, DC, in 1989. I wanted to find McKinsey's name first and approached a park ranger to expedite the process.

"Sir," I said, "help me find—"

I froze, as I am while I try to write this. I could not talk. I pointed to Mac's full name, which I had written on the back of a photo I carried of the detachment. The ranger led me to his name, chiseled on the black granite wall. I didn't want to look. Maybe he wasn't there—not dead. There it was, "Gerald L. McKinsey Jr." I stood at attention and held a salute for some time. I've never cried so much or for so long. I reached out and touched his name and said, "Hey, Mac. You're the best. We miss you."

History recorded January 21, 1968, as the beginning of the siege of Khe Sanh that lasted seventy days.

–15–

72-HOUR DAY

I feel like there is going to be a real battle, the largest ever, very soon. It will be in the Khe Sanh area. After what happened to us Black Cats on a simple resupply mission, they are able to see how strong the NVA are. There are reports of an enormous amount of NVA moving to that area. Even tanks from the north are heading in that direction. Secret Info!

— 23 JAN 68 Letter to Diane

The evening of January 31, 1968, before I had my meeting with the pilots, three of my Cat Killer buddies came into our hootch and talked briefly about their day. Petty, Cat Killer 2-4, came in from his recon flight and interrupted the conversation by saying, "Something must be coming. You won't believe what I saw. While flying cover for a convoy between Hue and Dong Ha, I saw about thirty Viet Cong flags flying over villages. I flew low over each one and didn't draw any fire."

"Have you reported this?" I asked.

"Yes, everybody in command knows."

During our meeting, I included Petty's report. We all agreed that things had felt different in our AO since January 1. Truscott came by the hootch and asked if he could take door gunners Brown, Payne, and McColon to bring in the M60s from the airfield.

"Go ahead," I said. "You think something is up also?"

"Yes, sir," he replied. "I'll report when we get back."

I ran into Desi outside my hootch. He told me his other two mates, Egan and Austier, were out conducting security, making him the only Aussie in the compound. We were all on edge.

Near midnight, Petty's crew chief came in to wake him. The crew chief told Petty to head out immediately and fly recon to detect any enemy movement.

Petty flew for three hours between Hue and Dong Ha. I woke up when he came back in at 3:00 a.m. and walked by my bunk. I asked him how it went out there, but another pilot, Lieutenant Harold, spoke up before he could answer.

"Petty, is there anything I should know before going out?" Harold was scheduled to fly next and was already putting on his flight suit and boots.

"Yeah," Petty said in an almost kidding tone. "Look for ten thousand NVA troops coming in on the north side of the Citadel."

At that instant, a rocket struck in the middle of the compound with a deafening crack. There had been no early warning siren, and the unexpected impact threw everything into confusion. I was suddenly floating eight feet in the air looking down at some guy on a bunk and yelling at him to grab his weapon and get to the bunker because the next rocket would be right on top of him. I was shouting at myself. My senses were scrambled, and nothing made sense. Somehow I found myself heading to the bunker near my hootch, and I was almost there when two more rockets landed in the compound.

The entrance to our bunker was only five feet away, but I was disoriented from the rockets. I found my way by instinct acquired from past attacks. Three Cat Killer pilots came rushing in behind me. We all had our M16s ready and pointed them outward through holes made for firing from the bunker. Muzzle flashes sparked in the surrounding terrain, but we had not fired our weapons yet. I fought to clear my head and refocus.

Flares lit the entire area, and we saw movement. We all started firing at once.

Incoming bullets struck everywhere around us. A loud explosion boomed to our left where Colonel Kelley's command bunker had a tower manned by an M60 machine gun, providing an elevated firing position. The tower seemed to explode. It must have taken a direct hit from an RPG. But after a pause, the machine gun started firing again. There was so much noise. The enemy was directly in front of us.

Two more explosions sounded, this time to our immediate right. I thought that had to be the warrants' bunker. Then the tower took another direct hit, and the machine gun fell silent.

We kept firing. The explosions right outside our well-fortified bunker were deafening. They had to be hand grenades. As bad as it seemed in front of us, the guys in the bunkers on both sides were taking more fire. Each time I put a fresh clip into my M16, I went to the bunker's entry to see if the enemy had broken through. I knew if they had, they could easily throw a satchel charge into our entryway and kill all of us. I told the other pilots what I was doing. I don't think they heard me. The noise and incredible amount of small-arms fire continued for two hours.

I was about to check the entryway again to scan for enemy movement in the eerie flare light floating down from above. I turned, and in that shadowy haze, I came face to face with someone. I froze, my mind screaming at my body to react, that the enemy had broken through, when the face spoke.

"Boss, we have been hit and hit hard."

It was Tom Pullen. He had blood all over his face.

"Tom, I have to get you to the infirmary," I said.

"I think I can make it. They need help in our bunker."

All I could think was that I had to help them. I went through the warrants' hootch to get to their bunker. I could see machine-gun fire originating from their fortification. As I started to enter, I saw Richard Gilmore slumped down, obviously wounded. Desi Ford was firing an old .30-caliber Browning model 1919 machine gun, swiveling it on its tripod. I didn't see any more of my men.

I lifted Gilmore and put his arm around my neck and took him to the infirmary. He didn't speak. He was in shock.

When we arrived, Dedrick was lying on his back on a metal gurney with his eyes closed. He shivered as if cold. Aye, Pullen, and Skulborstad were seated on the floor next to the wall.

"We got hit hard, Boss," Tom said. "Check Dedrick."

Dedrick was hardly breathing. Each intake of air was a gasp. I saw the doctor and got his attention. The doc was an MD, a captain in his early thirties who was obligated for two years of active duty. "Have you checked everyone?" I said. I knew that he had, but still I couldn't help asking.

"I have them stable," the doctor said, "the best I can for now."

I asked him to look at Gilmore and turned back to Dedrick. From six inches away, I spoke to him but got no response. In the dim light, I could not see where he had been hit, but I knew it was bad. I also knew I couldn't stay with him.

"I'm going back to the perimeter," I told my men. "I'll be back."

Right outside the door, I paused and sat down. I said a short prayer. There was nothing more I could do.

Machine-gun fire was nonstop. There was so much of it that we couldn't tell if it was incoming or outgoing. I went to the warrants' bunker to see if they needed more help. Four soldiers were still firing, and more ammo was coming in behind me. Desi was still firing the .30-caliber. The bunker, which had no top cover, looked half destroyed. It had taken at least three direct hits from RPGs.

I went back to the Cat Killers' bunker, and they were glad to see my M16 and me. Mortars started coming in on us, which probably kept the NVA from launching a ground attack since their mortars would have killed their own men.

During this kind of intense combat, everything turns fuzzy in your mind. The next thing I remember, it was 7:00 a.m., and I knew I had to get my men medevaced. They all seemed stable except Dedrick. He was still gasping for every breath but more slowly. A Marine H-46 Sea Knight was scheduled to come in and medevac all the WIAs. Within minutes, Truscott found me and gave me a report on the other crew chief and door gunner. He said that the newest crew chief and gunner needed to be medevaced. They were not wounded, but their ability to fight had shut down.

"Make sure to get Dedrick on the first helicopter," I said.

"You bet we will, Boss," he answered without hesitation.

The first marine helicopter was on its way in. Within minutes, my men had Dedrick strapped to a stretcher and placed on a jeep. Three vehicles left the compound headed for the Landing Ship Tank (LST) ramp on the Perfume River, which was about four winding city blocks away.

Fifty meters out of the compound gate, they encountered intense enemy fire. It was a firefight all the way. The LST ramp was the closest clearing for any helicopter to land. They loaded the wounded, and then the helicopter headed for Phu Bai.

When Truscott and the gunners returned, they said the next ship was inbound. They needed to get the rest of the pilots to the LST ramp immediately.

"How in the world did you make it?" I asked Truscott.

He said they had taken fire the entire way.

"Do you need me to provide more cover?" I said.

"We don't have room for anyone else, and, besides, you are the only pilot left. You can't go."

The second trip was just as bad as the first, but all of the pilots, crew chief, and door gunner were medevaced. The marine pilots completed their mission with their vulnerable H-46s. They did an outstanding job.

I was relieved once my men were medevaced. Seeing them severely wounded and having minimum care was really affecting me. Now I actually welcomed being on the perimeter and shooting the enemy. We were informed that the marines would need at least two more days to bring in reinforcements. There was continuous sniper fire, but we could stay low and move from bunker to bunker.

I sought out my combat-tested pal, Desi Ford. He had just opened a Pabst Blue Ribbon beer. I asked someone to take our picture. I told him if it was OK with him, I would stay close to him until this thing was over. He filled me in on how the warrants had been wounded. At times, he was the only one in their bunker firing to prevent the enemy from breaking through.

"Fordy, this can get bloody worse," he said. "There is a VC flag flying from the Citadel. They have taken it over."

We could see the flag flying about seven hundred meters away from us. I wanted to say something but was too scared to talk. I was dreading the fast-approaching night.

I sought out my pals, the forward air control pilots who had been in the same bunker with me. We sat outside protected from snipers, and one of them drank a beer. We all hoped the marines would make it from Phu Bai. We could hear a battle raging across the Perfume River. I thought that the first ARVN division under General Truong's command must have its hands full.

That night was a mixture of mortars, snipers, and flares. We were 100 percent on alert. There would be no sleep.

Sometime after midnight, we repelled a probing attack. One of the Cat Killers threw more than fifty hand grenades at the attackers. Most were effective, but ten of them hit overhead communications wire and landed five or ten feet in front of our bunker. The explosions gave us temporary blindness and concussions and destroyed about a third of our sandbags. No one knew this was happening until the daylight hours of the next day.

As morning broke and we were able to count, we found that our compound had sustained fifteen casualties, and thirty-six enemy had been killed outside our perimeter.

I do not remember much during the next day except for dreading the night. Word went through the compound that a full ground attack would happen on the third night, February 2. I told Des to stay close in case we were overrun and had to escape and evade. We made plans on the route we would take. We gathered ammo, and I'm sure I ate some C-rations, probably fruit cocktail, crackers, and peanut butter.

At some point, I decided to make a deal. "God," I prayed, "if you get me out of this, I will—" I stopped there, knowing the next words out of my mouth had better be something I could live up to. "I'll stay in shape. That's the best I can do."

About 3:00 a.m., Desi returned to my bunker after checking other defensive positions. He drew close and whispered, "Hey, Fordy, I just found out we got the bloody boogers right where we want them."

At last, I thought, *good news.*

Then he said, "The little bastards are all around us."

My insides felt as if they were clenched in a vise. I could only mutter, "Des, that's not funny."

"Sorry, mate, bad joke." He took up the position next to me.

When the predawn light finally came, I was glad to see it. Des was no longer beside me, but he returned from somewhere out of breath from moving fast.

"Hey, Fordy, want to shoot a sniper? I've got one located about three hundred meters out."

A shot of adrenaline hit me. "Yeah, where?"

We moved slowly to the southeastern corner of the compound next to the warrants' bunker. Desi pointed to two clumps of palm trees. We were under cover, and the dim light made both the sniper and us difficult targets. As I carefully looked over the sandbags, Des repeated three times to me where to shoot. Fatigue was making it hard to put words into action.

I put the selector switch on my M16 to semiautomatic. I had a full eighteen rounds of solid tracers in the magazine. I could feel myself shaking as I fired, but after three or four rounds, I knew every round could have been a kill shot. When all the rounds were expended, I eased down under cover.

Des patted me on my steel pot. "Good shooting, Fordy," he said, "but you shot the wrong tree."

I put another clip in with very shaky hands. We both shot the sniper.

By February 3, we had been on full alert from constant enemy pressure for three days and nights. I was still suffering the effects of a concussion, eating very little, and managing to function on no more than four hours of sleep. For the next few hours, I roamed the southeastern side of the compound, shooting at any suspected sniper location while standing upright in full view. I just didn't care.

The best targets were the windows of a two-story schoolhouse at a distance of 120 meters. That was a target that anybody could hit. I went through a lot of M16 ammo, which was in plentiful supply. No one suggested I take cover. I don't remember anyone moving around in the compound. I felt I was doing some good, and I was placing each round within twelve inches of where I wanted it. Suddenly there was a steady *boom, boom, boom* from a powerful weapon.

I knew instantly what it was. There was no mistaking that sound. To my right, between two hootches, a marine deuce and a half with a .50-caliber machine gun had opened up on the same schoolhouse I had been targeting. I had not seen or heard the truck. It had come through the front gate and made its way through the compound, then got in position to fire.

What a difference in firepower. In twenty minutes, the entire school was burned to the ground. What a good feeling. The marine reactionary force had broken through.

It had taken three days to fight their way five klicks from Phu Bai to our compound. This account was later depicted in the movie *Full Metal Jacket*. I went to the marines manning the .50-caliber and said, "Sure good to see you guys." Then I snapped off a silver-tipped incendiary round from the belt of their ammo, which I still have.

While I was reloading the seven empty magazines I carried for my M16, I was told that two Black Cat helicopters were coming to pick up medevacs and any 282nd survivors. I located Truscott and told him to find our gunners, get their gear together, and meet me by the front gate. A radioman told us our ships were thirty minutes out. We assembled on the steps of a two-story stucco building close to the front gate.

"We may get out," I said to the guys. "Let me take your picture."

I made them smile. I didn't think to include myself in the picture, but my M16 and gear are in the foreground.

When our Hueys were fifteen minutes out, we loaded up in a jeep, one of three headed that way. As soon as we left the compound, we started firing our weapons at suspected enemy positions and continued the entire four blocks. We saw muzzle flashes everywhere and I knew they were all directed at us. Shooting back toward the flashes was easy but not very accurate. When the first ship landed, I told the gunners and Truscott to get on with four or five wounded marines.

"Negative, sir," Truscott yelled over the noise. "I'll put on another marine, but I'm staying with you."

"OK, get them out of here," I said.

It made me proud that Truscott wanted to stay with me. I felt safer having this brave soldier at my side.

We were under constant enemy sniper fire, but we returned even more fire. The next ship came in with an Alley Cat escort. The big black cat on the nose was a welcome sight, though we were still far from safe.

As soon as it landed, I jumped on the toe of the left skid to identify the AC. I recognized Calvin Dennison by his almost-white eyebrows. He was staring at me, wide-eyed.

"My God, Lieutenant Ford, we thought you were dead," he said.

I got close and yelled the only thing I could think of. "Are you sure this thing will fly?"

I yelled the same thing that Captain Steiner had yelled to me on January 22 at Khe Sanh. I repeated it again before he could answer.

"Yeah, get on. We'll get you home."

At the 2013 Black Cat Reunion, Dennison spoke about that moment: "When we landed to pick up survivors, I saw two guys to my right—each on one knee, in the outer part of the landing zone. They were firing toward a university building with their M16s. Bullets were passing two feet in front of my windshield and appeared to be going directly into their chests. The two guys began running toward my ship. Those two, I soon discovered, were you [Ford] and Truscott. While all this was happening, I said a prayer. I promised God if he could get me out of this, I would never take a drink of alcohol again for the rest of my life." It was a promise he has kept.

I remember very little about the flight that day. I do know I hated being a passenger. Before we landed at Da Nang, I got the crew chief's helmet and asked Dennison over the intercom about my men.

"Well," he said, and then there was a long pause. He probably didn't want to be the one to tell me. "Dedrick didn't make it," he said at last. "I think the other pilots are still alive, but I don't know where they are."

I gave the helmet back without responding. I couldn't find any words.

When we landed, most of the company greeted us. As I exited the Huey, someone got close to my left ear and told me I had been listed as missing in action and he would personally make sure notification back to the US was stopped.

"How are the rest of the pilots?" I asked.

"Pullen and Skulborstad were the worst and taken to Japan. Gilmore and Aye were flown to the army hospital in Hawaii."

I nodded but didn't say anything else. I don't remember eating, taking a shower, or locating a bunk.

A day later, February 4, I was awakened and told I was needed to fly back to Hue. I was disoriented. I had to get up and go by supply to check out another flight helmet and chest protector. Mine had been destroyed during the first night of the attack.

I had to be ready to fly in twenty-four hours. I was going back into the battle.

–16–

BATTLE OF HUE

*No, the media doesn't help . . . always in the way and arrogant.
If they do have us take them to an LZ we know it won't be over
5 minutes before they will be screaming for us to come back and
pick them up. So they can get back to booze and air conditioners.
We would be better off without them.*

— 26 JAN 68 Letter to Diane

My first mission back into Hue began on February 6. That day and the next two were intense. Every minute of those days, I lived with the feeling that I might not survive.

I can't remember the name of any of my right-seat pilots. They were new and couldn't possibly have found any of our destinations flying low level. I was in it alone. There was no time to build trust, so these inexperienced pilots were there only to change the radio frequencies when I requested. With each one of them, I just dialed in Phu Bai ADF and told them that if I got shot, to follow the ADF needle to Phu Bai hospital.

"Do you understand?" I asked them. They confirmed, and those were probably the only words we spoke to one another each day. I never let them touch the controls. In less than a year, I had become the old man.

On February 6, we had one-mile visibility and a three-hundred-foot ceiling. We loaded up with medical supplies, took off from Marble Mountain, and low leveled around Da Nang Bay. We paralleled the coast three hundred meters out feet wet. I had the door gunners clear their weapons once, and then knowing we would encounter a determined enemy, I had them clear their weapons two more times.

"Be ready to fire as soon as we are over dry land," I cautioned.

I turned inland for the ten-minute flight to Hue. Within three minutes, we started hearing enemy gunfire, and the door gunners immediately returned fire from both sides of the aircraft. I had my pilot dial in the contact frequency and let them know I was within five minutes inbound to the First ARVN Division hospital pad. The radio operator was a female Vietnamese soldier who had coordinated hundreds of missions for us in the past. She said, "2-1, I'm glad you made it through the attack. We are surrounded. We sure need your help."

I chose to come in from the east where there was less cover for the enemy. The preferred invading route for the NVA was from the north and the west. The attack on our compound had come from the southeast. I planned to exit south, flying the route the marines had cleared in their assault toward Hue.

Gunfire was sporadic until one klick from Hue, and then it became more sustained. From hours of experience flying low level in enemy territory, I knew we would be a difficult target as long as our gunners returned fire.

I called the hospital pad and advised them I was just a minute from them. We would be flying over the outer walls of the Citadel soon, so I advised the gunners to be prepared to cease fire. As soon as I saw the outer wall, I bottomed the collective to slow the Huey and gave the order to cease fire.

When we landed, ARVN soldiers off-loaded the medical supplies. A marine was waving his arms to get our attention, so I picked up and hovered to the east end of the medevac pad. He climbed onto the toe of the skid and asked if we could help them. They were fighting alongside the Vietnamese, he said, and he needed to get his wounded out. I told him to put them on and we would take them to Phu Bai. As they loaded the four marines, I asked him if he wanted me to come back for him. He said to call him after we had unloaded his men. He gave me his contact frequency, and I wrote it down on the Plexiglas windshield. My pilot dialed it in, and we did a communications check.

"This is Black Cat 2-1. How do you read?" I called.

A marine had appeared to our right with a PRC-25 and replied, "We copy loud and clear."

Over the intercom, I said, "Are we clear? Coming up."

I exited the same way I came in, and, after flying one klick, I turned southeast. I called Phu Bai and told them I was five minutes north. We requested direct clearance to the hospital pad.

"Clear, direct 2-1, you are the only aircraft in the area," Phu Bai said.

With that news, I remember thinking that if we were to go down, the chances of anyone finding us were not good.

Stretchers were ready when we arrived at the hospital pad. As the wounded were unloaded, a marine major jumped on our skid. He was obviously stressed but in control. I took off my helmet to make sure I could hear him. He yelled that they needed us back at Hue and asked if we would take some ammo. During his urgent request, he was pointing one hundred meters from the medevac pad to a stack of wooden ammunition boxes.

"Yes, sir," I said.

I started getting light on the skids, picked it up, and started hovering toward the ammo. He just stayed on the skids and reached his arm in the open window for stability.

The major performed the important task of ensuring the ammo was distributed properly to prevent overloading the Huey. We performed a power check by lifting up to a three-foot hover to make sure the load wasn't too heavy. I saw this fine officer many times during the remainder of February.

We took off toward Hue maintaining low level and a slightly different route. Ground fire was more severe. I had a good feeling about our gunners though. After surviving the first hour, they were handling their job better.

At Hue, the marines unloaded the ammo at the medevac pad at the Citadel and then loaded four wounded marines. Over the radio, the marine in the loading zone I had talked to earlier said they should be good now.

We low leveled back to Phu Bai. While the wounded were being unloaded, I recognized the major who had jumped on our skid.

"2-1, be advised there is going to be a POL set up on the coast with the call sign Omaha Beach," he said. "It should be in service tomorrow. Are you coming back?"

"If you need me, I'll be back, sir. Do you know how to contact me?"

"Affirmative. I know who you are. Here is the contact frequency for Omaha Beach POL."

He held up his hand with the frequency written on his palm. I wrote the numbers on the windshield, as well as on the front of my SOI. We had enough fuel to get back to Da Nang.

The next two days were even more intense than the first, and flying single ship with inexperienced copilots was affecting me. By the time I landed at company headquarters, I had flown twenty-five missions into the battle in three days.

Early in the morning of February 9, I was given a mission to lead a flight of four Hueys into the Citadel for an emergency resupply. The marines were still waging a major battle and were running low on ammunition and supplies. I briefed the other three ACs on the route I was going to take and what to expect. They trusted me to lead them and said so.

As we walked to the aircraft, a major from headquarters stepped up beside me and nervously stated, "I am flying right seat." I had a sinking feeling. The last thing I needed was an inexperienced pilot who might not take orders.

After leaving the coast, we immediately took heavy fire. We were low leveling toward Phu Bai with less than one mile of visibility. The major started screaming over the intercom, "We are taking fire, we are taking fire, we're hit, we're hit. Do you know where you are going? Do you know where you are going?"

"Yes, sir," I emphatically replied. "Stay off the intercom. I have to call Phu Bai."

We landed at Phu Bai in trail formation, and took on ammo and supplies. While the supplies were being loaded, I looked over at the major. He was staring down at his feet. I started to say something over the intercom but decided against it. I couldn't believe I had such a scared old man in the cockpit with me.

As soon as we left Phu Bai and headed for Hue in trail formation, two of the aircraft sustained hits. We stayed in formation as I led them to the hospital pad inside the Citadel.

During my earlier briefing, I had told all the ACs it would be difficult to land four helicopters in the hospital LZ, but each did a good job. The last ship hovered back about thirty meters to be unloaded. This allowed enough space between the rest of us to rotate 180 degrees and hover to wait our turn. After we had all unloaded, they were instructed to navigate back to the coast and return to Da Nang. My ship was the last to be unloaded, and I took off right away.

The other aircraft ahead of us were reporting intense fire. We all took hits. Two reported that they might have to go down. The major pushed the intercom button on the floor and yelled, "Do you know which way you are going? How are you going to get out of here? Tell your door gunners to fire."

The door gunners were already firing, and his panicked transmission interrupted the flow of information from the other ships, breaking my concentration. I flew up to about thirty feet, pressed my left leg against the collective and held the cyclic with my left hand, then reached over and turned off the volume on his radio. He had raised his knees to his chest in a fetal position.

I picked up a transmission from one of the ships that they were making a precautionary landing on the coast. I knew I could find them in two minutes and pick up the crew, but before I did, they decided to fly back to Da Nang. I made sure all ships were en route home. When we cleared the coast, I headed south toward Da Nang and told the gunners they did a good job. They were probably concentrating so much that they didn't hear the major's panicked voice over the intercom.

Coming in on short final, I turned the intercom volume back up and told the major that I was glad we made it. He kept his head down and did not answer. I hovered into a revetment and told the major I would take care of shutdown and fill out the logbook. The door gunner helped him out of the aircraft. I don't remember ever seeing him again.

The other three ACs met me in front of my aircraft, and they said that it was a good thing I knew where I was going.

"You did a heck of a job navigating," one of them said. "We were all lucky to make it. I hope we never go back."

I told them they had done a good job—which they had.

I walked to my hootch, sat down on my bunk, and put my head down between my legs. My nerves were getting the best of me. I'm not sure how long I sat with my head in my hands, elbows on my knees, eyes closed. I felt dizzy, so I opened my eyes and looked at the floor to make sure it wasn't moving. Someone's boots stood right in front of me. I sat up and saw a blurry figure.

"Lieutenant Ford, you have to go back," he said quietly.

I asked, "How long have you been standing there?"

"Not long, sir—maybe five minutes."

I simply knew my luck had run out. I was overwhelmed by the feeling that this time I would not make it. The next thing I remember is approaching the aircraft light headed, nauseated, and so scared I could see the M16 shaking in my right hand. Tears welled up in my eyes. I could not believe what was happening to me. *I'm an aircraft commander with hundreds of missions under my belt*, I thought. *I've been through everything, including a three-day ground attack.*

I stopped for a moment to steady myself. I was completely alone and could not hear a sound. Dizziness began to overtake me, and I thought my knees were going to buckle. It felt as if I were going to fall off a cliff. I didn't want anyone to see me in this condition and knew I had to figure something out fast.

Then an idea struck me. I started walking slowly toward the second platoon hootch, trying to maintain a confident posture. It looked so far away. I reasoned that if I could take another experienced aircraft commander with me, I could make it. I was within ten steps of the hootch when I knew exactly who I wanted to come along.

Everyone looked at me as if death were standing in the doorway. I mustered up a firm voice.

"I want another aircraft commander to go with me—Colburn."

Instantly Colburn clearly said, "I'll go with you, Boss."

I was surprised and glad that he called me Boss. It instantly lifted my spirits. Colburn had never been with the Hue detachment, and we had not flown together since before we both made AC seven months ago on September 13, 1967. We had maintained a lot of respect for one another.

Colburn quickly gathered his flight helmet, chest protector, and .45-caliber pistol and was walking beside me within a few seconds. I did not have to tell him how bad our mission was going to be. He knew, and so did our crew chief and gunner. They were ready. We hovered to the runway for takeoff clearance. I keyed the mic. Nothing came out of my mouth. I tried again. My voice had shut down.

"Black Cat 2-1, is that you?" the tower operator asked.

I keyed the mic twice for affirmative, relieved I didn't have to talk.

"You're cleared. No traffic," the tower said and then backed up the clearance by aiming a green spotlight at us.

We took off and stayed low level. I tried to speak without keying the mic. On the third or fourth attempt, a sound finally came out. I practiced a few simple words before I was ready to transmit.

"Hey, Bart, thanks for coming," I said. "Having you in the right seat makes a big difference."

"Tell me what you need. I'll stay close," he said.

I knew exactly what he meant. It gave me assurance that he would be ready to change frequencies and most importantly, be ready to take the controls if I got shot.

We took enormous fire within four hundred meters of leaving the coastline. The weather now provided only half-mile visibility. I gained confidence with Colburn in the right seat and flew lower and faster. Our gunners never stopped firing until we reached Phu Bai.

The same efficient marine major helped load our aircraft, and in one minute, we cleared ourselves and were on our way to resupply the marines inside the Citadel. We took two hits en route, but they didn't strike any main component of the Huey. No warning light came on. Colburn, as expected, was calm. What a relief it was to know he was there.

After unloading, we took medevacs to Phu Bai, but en route they radioed us to return. More wounded were arriving in fifteen minutes. While the hospital personnel unloaded our wounded, one of the gunners said, "Sir, you won't believe what happened." Colburn and I looked back at him. It surprised both of us because neither one of our gunners had spoken the entire flight. He told us two tracers had passed through the cargo section right behind our heads. It's possible that every fifth round is a tracer, which meant that six or more rounds could have zipped through without hitting anyone or anything.

"Keep firing and make them keep their heads down," I said. "We clear? Coming up."

I acted as if this were normal even as I wondered how we could survive another mission.

We completed four more. When we got released, we flew to Omaha Beach to refuel. The twenty-minute fuel warning light had been on for about seven minutes. While refueling, a Marine Mule flatbed vehicle used to transport ammo and supplies drove up with three wounded. We did not hesitate. We stopped refueling and loaded the marines. We had put at least four hundred pounds of fuel on by then, which was plenty to get those guys to Phu Bai.

After unloading the wounded in Phu Bai, Colburn called Omaha to ask if they needed us. We got a negative and a thanks. We had enough fuel to get home.

I felt much better on the way back to headquarters. I was back to my old self. Bart and I talked about how many we had medevaced and how there was no letup in the fire we had encountered. We both thanked our gunners. They were outstanding. I noted that it seemed as though we had evacuated as many lieutenants as we had PFCs. The lieutenants must have been leading the fight.

During shutdown, we found two bullet holes in our aircraft—one in the horizontal stabilizer and the other right through a tail rotor blade. We were surprised that the hole in the tail rotor was clean and that the bullet had not inflicted more damage since the rotor spins at more than sixteen hundred RPM. It just seemed impossible.

Previously I had taken hits twice on the main rotor blade, and both times they had left big, gaping holes about eight feet out on the blade and caused moderate vibration throughout the aircraft. The skin had peeled all the way back, exposing the inner aluminum honeycomb. The crew chief, after shutdown, pulled the skin back into place, then wrapped five rounds of duct tape around it, went eight feet out on the opposite blade and wrapped it five rounds also to balance it. We cranked the thing back up. It felt smooth and flew four or five more missions.

Over the next ten days, Colburn and I took hits every time we flew. None of the hits kept us from completing our missions, but one came close. While resupplying a small outpost that was surrounded in the southwest housing section of Hue, we had to fly at a vulnerable four hundred feet as we tried to locate them. Any higher and we would have been in the clouds and lost visual contact with the ground.

We took a hit in the forty-two-degree gearbox, which diverts the drive shaft from the engine forty-two degrees up to the tail rotor. The hit caused the Huey to vibrate violently and plummet three hundred feet. The controls were useless.

Solid muzzle flashes were visible below, and the sound of automatic weapons came toward us. Our gunners never stopped firing. At one hundred feet, I got some sluggish control back and spotted yellow smoke.

"I got yellow smoke," I transmitted.

"Affirmative yellow," the outpost radioed back. "We are taking incoming mortars."

But I was already committed to the landing zone. We were five feet above the ground on short final when a mortar round exploded under our aircraft. The nose went straight up. I pushed the cyclic forward to level the aircraft and land.

As we put the skids on the ground, the gunners and a passenger who came to help unload threw the ammo and supplies out onto the LZ. Two more mortars landed within twenty feet of us, but the surrounding damaged buildings kept the shrapnel from hitting us.

We exited and stayed low level, flying toward Omaha Beach to refuel. The vibration subsided as we headed that way. After we landed, we started to shut down to assess the damage but got a call that we needed to pick up an air force forward air control pilot at the LST ramp. He needed to be flown to ARVN headquarters inside the Citadel to coordinate much needed air strikes. Once there, we were to pick up more wounded.

We took the risk that the aircraft was flyable and, after pumping in needed fuel, took off. A description of this mission to pick up the air force officer, Lt. Col. Richard L. Brown, whom I had seen several times at the Hue Airfield and in the MACV Compound, is described in his book *Palace Gate*.

Lt. Col. Brown described waiting for us at the LST ramp and observing how intense the fighting was on the other side of the river between the pickup LZ and ARVN headquarters. While we were on short final to the LST ramp, he noted how rounds were zipping all around him, in what we called "a hot LZ." It took him only a few seconds to get on, and I pulled in full power while he belly-flopped into the cargo section. I accelerated so rapidly he said he could only roll over and sit up while grabbing some nylon straps.

After crossing low over the Perfume River, we hit a couple of palm trees and cleared the rooftops of buildings by two feet. I flew a short circular route to the ARVN HQ, and my passenger observed the enemy firing at us out of doorways and on rooftops. I could see muzzle flashes everywhere.

When I landed, he ran out in front of the Huey and gave us what he described as a salute "with feeling."

Lt. Col. Brown summarized his ninety-second flight as an adventure, with flying that took skill, guts, and a cool head. The helicopter crew, he wrote, had probably looked on this short flight as an errand. He noted that people could get used to anything, and he hoped we all survived. His statements were appreciated.

★★★★

Having Bart Colburn in the cockpit with me during the Battle of Hue was a lifesaver. Together we flew twenty-five hours and sixty-two missions into the battle. We encountered constant, heavy enemy fire and flew low level in lousy weather every minute. There is no way to know how many wounded we medevaced or how many enemy we shot or how many supplies and how much ammunition we delivered. We did not try. It had to be a lot of each. Our gunners came through as expected, as did our aircraft. Colburn was solid. He made me confident, aggressive, and better. We completed every mission.

After our last mission and the aircraft shut down, we took off our helmets, stayed in the cockpit, and talked. We were almost jovial and reminded one another that we had earned our flight pay. We were thankful to be alive and proud to have gotten each other through. Then Colburn said, "Can you believe we made it?"

I do not remember sleeping or eating the last ten days Colburn and I flew together. I only remember being in the cockpit.

I later learned that when Colburn got out of the cockpit on February 19, the day we flew our last mission together, he took an assignment in maintenance to test-fly aircraft. He flew very little until he went home in mid-April. I would see him eight months later when we were both instructor pilots at Fort Wolters, Texas, and he had just been married.

Midafternoon of February 19, our company executive officer told me I needed to go to the Da Nang morgue to identify Dwight Dedrick, whose body had to go through an official identification procedure before being sent home to his family. I asked the officer to check out a jeep for me and to have someone find Truscott. I knew Truscott could provide security for the jeep ride, as well as help me identify Dedrick.

We drove the three-mile roundabout way from our headquarters to the air force base in Da Nang, which we called Da Nang main, where the morgue was located. We saw few people on our way but kept our weapons ready. Each of us had an M16 and a sidearm. Truscott drove the jeep.

When we entered the morgue, the formaldehyde smell was strong. There were more than eighty zipped-up black body bags placed on gurneys in orderly rows. A medical type with no rank showing on his white lab coat directed us to two separate bags. He unzipped each and asked if the soldiers were Dedrick. I gave him a definite negative on both. Then he unzipped a bag and exposed Dedrick's head and shoulders.

After two weeks, it was difficult to recognize this young, energetic, humorous, brave friend. I knew I was fortunate to have had the chance to serve with him, but all I could think of right then was his parents and their grief. Dedrick's freshly grown reddish mustache helped us make the positive ID. I was asked three times to confirm. Truscott backed up my positive ID each time.

The next day, February 20, I boarded a plane destined for R&R in Hawaii and my first wedding anniversary with Diane.

–17–

R&R

I've been here about seven months. This has gone pretty fast so far. I've got a job that has a real purpose. We are doing a job that a whole helicopter company should be doing.

==== 27 JAN 68 Letter to Mom, Dad, and Bill

Sometime in mid-January, I called Diane on the Military Affiliate Radio System (MARS) line. MARS was the only way to communicate by voice back to the States. It was run by the military in coordination with civilians on the high-frequency radio band. We were limited to two calls per year for five minutes each, and we had to schedule any call at least two weeks in advance. Communication with another person on the MARS line was like transmitting over the radio in combat—only one person could talk at a time. When one party was finished talking, that person had to say, "Over." This allowed the MARS operator to move a toggle switch so the other party could respond.

I called Diane to make sure all the arrangements were made for her to be in Hawaii when I arrived. This was the first time I had talked to her since I had left the States seven months before. Since she had never talked over a radio, the conversation was really quite comical. When the MARS operator had us both ready, he said, "OK, Lieutenant, start your transmission."

"Hi, sweetheart," I said. "Sure looking forward to our first anniversary in Hawaii. Is everything set? Over."

She responded, "Hi, over."

"Hi, hon, it's good to hear your voice. Bring me a few civilian clothes. I am sure looking forward to seeing you. Is everything ready? Over."

She responded, "Hi, Bob, over."

Our back-and-forth continued like that until we had about one minute left. To be sure to get a response to my last question, I said, "Diane, you need to answer with a little more detail. Now, do you have your plane ticket and has the hotel confirmed our reservation? Over."

She responded, "Yes. I'll be there. Over."

With that, the time was up, and we both hung up. I had to laugh at my obviously nervous wife of few words, but I was sure everything would go well.

On February 20, I put on my travel khaki uniform and flew on a C-130 to Chu Lai to out-process for R&R. I then boarded a Pan American 707 airline and flew nonstop to Hawaii.

We landed about 2:00 a.m. and were bused to Fort DeRussy to meet those who had come from the States. I was the first one off the bus. There were about thirty people, mostly female, waiting for loved ones. I quickly scanned the small gathering but did not see Diane.

I started to walk into a waiting area when this pretty girl walked up to me. "Hi, Bob," she said. "It's me."

I didn't recognize her. I can't explain why. Maybe it was all that had happened in the last seven months. Maybe I just couldn't believe I was in a secure area.

After a long hug, we started six wonderful days of getting reacquainted. Due to my late arrival, our room at the Hilton Hawaiian Village had been given away. The hotel manager quickly gave us the penthouse suite at the same rate. Our suite overlooked an unoccupied

Waikiki beach, with Diamondhead in the distant background. Early the next day, we stood on the balcony and talked for hours. It was a clear, cool, windless morning and such a beautiful setting.

The next three days, I completely forgot about the war as we walked the beach, went to Sea World Park, enjoyed a Harlem Globetrotters game, and had a front-row dinner table to see Don Ho. I remember a wonderful thought that crossed my mind and put a big smile on my face. I shared it with Diane. "What if when I get home in July," I asked her, "you are five months pregnant?"

I called home to Shawnee at a predesignated day and time to talk to my folks. My dad answered the phone and said he heard that things had been kind of rough where I was the last month. I said, "Yes, sir, it was, but I am OK."

"Let me tell you something, ol' buddy," he said, and then carefully spelled A-F-R-I-C-A.

I had no idea what he was trying to communicate. "Dad, what do you mean?"

He slowly spelled out A-F-R-I-C-A again. I still did not understand his line of thought. "A-F-C what?"

"Africa, Africa," he said. "I am going to Africa on a safari."

The only thing I could think to say was, "That's great, Dad. I'm sure you will have a good time. I'll look forward to some pictures when I get home." Then I asked him if I could talk to Mom.

My mom got on the phone and said, "Well, hi there. Did you get the cookies and fudge I sent?"

"Cookies? No—well, maybe I did. I think so. When did you send them?"

"I sent those cookies over three weeks ago. You should have received them by now. Didn't you get them?"

I knew I should do something to make her feel good, so I said, "Mom, I'm sure I did. I just don't remember. Nobody received much mail or packages last month."

"Well, if you are not getting my packages, I just won't send any."

"Mom, I bet I'll get your next batch, and they will be just great. I'll share them with all the pilots."

"Well, we will see," she said.

"I hope to see you in July, and tell brother Bill, Anne, and Peggo hi," I said, then added, "By the way, don't expect Diane to have a tan."

After we all said good-bye, Diane and I laughed about the last thing I said and wondered if Mom and Dad got it. That has provided a chuckle for us to this day.

While I was in Hawaii, I also called Tripler Army Medical Center to confirm that two of my men, John Aye and Richard Gilmore, were still patients. They were, so Diane and I drove our rented '67 Camaro out to see them. Tripler was a large, pink stucco hospital set up on elevated terrain. Diane began to push her fingernails on her cuticles as if to manicure them, so I knew she was nervous about going inside.

"Are you sure it's OK for me to go with you?" she asked. "I can stay in the car."

"No, come on. Go with me. I want you to meet my men."

Anyone would have been nervous. When we first entered, we could see rows of beds in the hallways full of wounded soldiers. An orderly escorted us to the second floor where Aye and Gilmore were located. We passed hundreds of wounded soldiers on the way. Each would have been overjoyed to have a conversation with me and for sure Diane. She whispered to me that they all seemed lonely and looked so thin.

As we approached Aye and Gilmore, Gilmore smiled but was quiet and subdued. Aye couldn't believe I was there. With boyish excitement, he said, "Boss, Boss, it's you. Thanks for coming. Great to see you!"

All the wounded soldiers around us became silent, wanting to hear every word the four of us said. We stayed at least two hours. Gilmore showed us a piece of jagged metal from the RPG attack on January 31. It was about half the size of a little finger and had been taken out of his chest a quarter-inch from his heart or, as he said, "from my ticker." Aye was back to himself, talking nonstop, and Diane was perfect. She never stopped smiling at everyone. All the soldiers looked at her like she was a movie star.

I was relieved after seeing my men. I knew they were going to make it.

After five days, my mind was already back in the cockpit. I wanted to get back and finish my tour. The obligation I felt to the men on the ground was strong. I wanted to smoke a cigarette.

On day six, Diane and I said good-bye at the airport. There were no emotional displays. We knew, though, that we had experienced something special. With a hug, we both said, "I'll see you in July."

The thought that I might not make it home never crossed my mind.

–18–

FIRST WEEK BACK

The VC put about 15–20 rockets right in on us my first night back in Da Nang. Luckily our intelligence reports were good, and we all were in the bunkers before they hit. Otherwise many people would have been hurt. About five rockets landed just 50 meters away from my bunker, but the five-foot-thick pile of sandbags stopped all of the shrapnel. The attacks here are nothing to compare with the one at Hue.

———————————————— 11 MAR 68 Letter to Diane

The day after I returned from R&R, I flew my first mission back to the Hue AO, and, as it would be 90 percent of the time, I flew single ship. It was the first time I had seen Hue from altitude since the Tet Offensive and the Battle of Hue. Tet—one of the largest military campaigns of the Vietnam War—was launched on January 31, 1968, the eve of the Vietnamese celebration of the Lunar New Year. There had been a prior agreement to cease fire during the celebrations, and it was broken by the Viet Cong and NVA. The Battle of Hue was considered one of the most devastating. We fought against fifteen thousand well-armed, trained, and highly motivated soldiers of the North Vietnamese Army. To relieve us at the MACV Compound and take back the city of Hue, marines were committed to the battle. During the first three days of Tet, the NVA executed over 2,800 civilians. The battle had taken a terrible toll on this beautiful city. The entrance into the old imperial

Citadel was rubble, as was as every foot of the ancient wall surrounding it. The entire infrastructure of Hue had been destroyed.

When we landed at the airfield to pick up some MACV advisors, we saw what was left of our two aircraft—scorched components and melted metal. After picking up the advisors, we took them to different outposts that included Quang Tri, Dong Ha, and other locations along the DMZ. It felt good to fly in favorable weather. We called it "severe clear."

Earlier that day, I had enjoyed the weather as I flew my semiannual check ride, which was scheduled for an hour but took only thirty minutes. Tom Woehl, the previous company standardization pilot, had DEROSed the previous December, and the new SIP was an outstanding pilot—it was my old pal Lennis Lee. I had not seen him much in the five and a half months since he had recommended me for my AC orders. I had been at Hue the entire time. Lennis kind of apologized about putting me through the check ride after the hours of combat I had flown, and I complimented him on earning this position in our unit. The check ride went well but when it was over, I didn't want to get out of the cockpit—I just wanted to sit and talk with my respected friend and listen to that North Carolina accent. I don't remember seeing Lennis very much before his DEROS a month later.

After delivering the MACV advisors later that day, we flew in support of an operation that was in contact with the enemy. En route I recognized a landmark: two tall, isolated trees. Many times in the past, we flew low level between them for the challenge and just for fun. They were close enough together that the main rotor blade would clip the branches of both trees. Although it had been well before Tet when I had last done this, I lined everything up perfectly.

Within fifty feet of the two trees, going about ninety knots, I suddenly saw a thin, black WD-1 communication wire stretched between them. The wire was at eye level and connected to a black cloth-covered pack about the size of a five-gallon water can. It was halfway up the tree on our right. We were committed, no chance to change our route. I knew I was in serious trouble.

In less than a second, we struck the commo wire. I gripped the cyclic and thought, *My God, have I screwed up! This is it!*

We flew through, snapping the wire. I thought I heard an explosive roar and that we were all being blown into a million tiny pieces. I was dead and glad it didn't hurt. Actually nothing happened. With relief, I made a fast cyclic climb to about three hundred feet and did a 180-degree turn. My copilot had not seen the wire. I had the door gunner, who had seen the potential explosive charge, fire into it with his M60. He was sure he hit the object several times, but it did not detonate. I decided not to go take a closer look.

We flew well over two hours for the operation. In addition to resupplying and medevacing WIAs, we also provided close fire support. On the way back to pick up our advisors, we paralleled a tree line at low level for about a minute. I was aware we should cross it as soon as possible to keep from being an easy target. In enemy territory, flying along a tree line was like being a moving duck in a shooting gallery. We did a sharp ninety-degree turn. As we crossed the tree line, a tremendous amount of gunfire erupted right beneath us. It had to be a large NVA unit.

We took only two hits because my gunners immediately returned accurate fire. I realized we were overmatched. A warning light flashed on the control panel, but we had to fly at least a klick before we could check things out. It was the twenty-minute fuel warning light, but I knew we had plenty of fuel, so I figured one of the hits must have set off the sensor. I climbed to one thousand feet, called for any Cat Killer, and asked if they had any fast movers in the area or if they could get some immediate artillery. While making the call, we closely observed where the enemy was concentrated by looking for muzzle flashes. We were out of range of any small arms, but a unit that size could have a Russian-made .51-caliber machine gun and easily engage us.

One of my Cat Killer buddies responded, "Negative fast movers. Negative artillery."

By that time, I had pinpointed on the map the enemy's location, so I pleaded with the Cat Killer.

"You have to find somebody. We could kill a bunch of bad guys."

He came back and said he had to go refuel but asked if I wanted to try naval gunfire and, if I did, to be ready to copy their frequency.

"Affirmative copy," I answered.

I wrote the frequency on the windshield with my black grease pencil and gave them a call, identifying myself as Black Cat 2-1. I said I had a fire mission and asked if they would accept. The navy guy probably thought I was a Cat Killer or some other forward air controller. I told them the coordinates of the enemy and asked for a marker. This was probably a first for any army helicopter pilot to direct naval gunfire.

"Roger, Black Cat 2-1. Say again the location of your target?" he said enthusiastically.

My gosh, I thought. *I am going to pull this off.*

Within two minutes, the naval fire controller said, "Marker out."

A few seconds later, we heard him say "Splash," and we saw the impact of the white-phosphorous marking round. It was relatively close to the enemy but needed to shift two hundred meters down and three hundred meters left.

"Roger, confirm Willie Pete," I transmitted. "From marker, down two left three. Fire for effect."

I couldn't believe how quick and accurate these guys were. They fired, and the whole area where we had encountered the enemy erupted.

"Good shooting. Repeat," I said, which meant put another volley of rounds into the same location. I'm not sure how many navy guns had fired, but it was impressive since I assumed they were firing from at least five miles away. They fired another volley, but this time when the controller said "Splash," I didn't observe any impact. I thought I had missed it, so once again I said, "Repeat." After another "splash" came from the navy guy, I still didn't observe any explosions. I wondered if our communications were interrupted. Did they think the fire mission had been terminated? I also wondered if they were firing long. These guns fired projectiles weighing as much as 2,700 pounds at speeds as fast as 2,690 feet per second with a range up to twenty-four miles. They could inflict major damage. We sure didn't want to get blown out of the sky by a stray round from these big guns, so I decided we had better end this now on a good note.

"Good shooting, Navy, ten unconfirmed KIA. Disengaging and changing frequency at this time. Black Cat 2-1 out."

With fuel running low, we were on our way to pick up the advisors and deliver them to the ARVN division headquarters at Hue, then would head back to Da Nang. I later found out that I had directed the firepower of the USS *Newport News*—a ship well known for its accuracy.

After shutdown, my crew chief inspected the aircraft for damage and discovered one round had penetrated a self-sealing fuel cell that had set off the twenty-minute warning light.

While I was walking to the operation's hootch, the company executive officer stopped me and asked in a formal way if I wanted to escort Dedrick's body back to the States. A picture of Dedrick formed in my mind—confident, calm, smiling, and tired. I could not see myself performing that duty, and I knew Dedrick would understand.

I imagined him saying his favorite expression. "Ye gads, Boss, you are the only one left of the Hue pilots. You gotta' stay. Who else could fly low level in bad weather in our AO? McKinsey and I will catch up with you later."

"No, sir," I told the officer. "Negative escort."

As it turned out, Dedrick and McKinsey did catch up with me later. I hadn't seen their faces for the last time.

–20–

ARTICLE 15

No matter how bad the weather, we seem to always get where we are going. I've already had 10 emergency medevacs and afterward wondered how in the world I ever found them. The clouds are right on the deck and a continuous rain. I've taken hits two different occasions yesterday—getting shot at going in low is getting common. Today I was going in to a LZ for three emergency medevacs, and the troops on the ground started screaming on the radio to break off, that I was taking automatic weapons fire. All I did was, after the break, came in 90 degrees from the source of fire and took the wounded out.

——————— 14 MAR 68 Letter to Mom, Dad, and Bill

During the remaining four and a half months of my tour, I remember the names of four new pilots—Meola, Culp, Stutsman, and Riley. The closeness I had with the earlier Hue detachment pilots was gone. Most of the time, we flew missions that had become routine: resupply, medevacing wounded—which was mostly under enemy fire—and providing close fire support. All of my missions were still in northern I Corps and originated from Da Nang.

Each morning about six, I told the crew we would start early and end early. I had heard some old sergeant say that—the same type who, when passing out mail, would remind young soldiers who did not get a letter from home that "you gotta write'em to get'em." We never ended early though. We always got back to headquarters at night, too late for company mess, so I would go to the officers' club after reporting into operations and have hard-boiled eggs that had been preserved in a gallon jar of cloudy pickle juice, along with a couple of polish sausages floating in brine. I nicknamed them "donkey patoots." I would wash them down with water or a fifteen-cent can of Schlitz, Lone Star, or Balentine beer. After eating C-rations all day, it wasn't so bad.

We played ping-pong on a table set up in a separate area of the officers' club. Three songs I remember on the jukebox were "To Sir With Love," "Young Girl," and "San Francisco." When I hear these songs, they really take me back there. I never lost at ping-pong unless a certain marine full colonel visited. He had heard I would be a challenge. At least three nights a week, he walked in, took off his jungle fatigue shirt, looked over at me, and nodded, which meant, "Let's play."

I never saw him talk to anyone else or drink a beer. The only conversation we had was to say the score or compliment each other on a good shot. Playing against him made me much better, yet at my best, he still beat me six out of ten times. The colonel was a gruff, burly guy who reminded me of the actor Ed Asner.

One morning before a nonemergency mission, just as I was getting into the cockpit, I was told that one of my door gunners, Payne, had been given an Article 15. He was to appear before a court-martial board in an hour at battalion headquarters. An Article 15 is a nonjudicial punishment proceeding. He was one of my Hue detachment door gunners and was with me during Tet. It sure got my attention. I immediately put my mission on hold because I wanted to testify.

On the way to the battalion headquarters, I learned that Payne had not returned from an Australian R&R on time and had stayed three unauthorized days. Five staff officers were in the small courtroom.

The highest rank was a lieutenant colonel. They had been assigned to determine punishment on several Article 15s that day.

I thanked them for letting me testify on behalf of this fine soldier, and then I addressed the ranking officer and told him in detail how Payne had always performed his duty. He had kept me and the crew alive every mission he had served as a volunteer door gunner. I emphasized how he had performed magnificently during the three-day siege at Hue in the MACV Compound. The board listened intently. I had their full attention.

I concluded by telling the board that when Payne left these proceedings, he would continue to perform his duty. "I will trust him with my life. Thank you. Do you have any questions?"

The ranking officer slowly looked to his left and right. "No, Lieutenant. You are excused."

I glanced at Payne as I left the room, and he looked like a soldier both thankful and relieved. I found out later that he was not punished.

—20—

BATTALION STAFF

My missions haven't changed any because I am flying north every time I get in the air. I wanted it that way because I know I can get much more accomplished than a pilot not knowing the area as well. Some of the politicians back home should come over and sit through even a small rocket attack. I would like to have one in the cockpit with me when I fly a normal mission—especially when I go north of Dong Ha or to another hot area. I landed in the middle of a firefight at Ba Long.

—————— 23 MAR 68 Letter to Mom, Dad, and Bill

When we didn't have passengers or medevacs and were not loaded with supplies, we entertained ourselves in various ways. One was to fly over any person or vehicle as low and fast as possible. If any of these "targets" were moving into the wind, they could not hear us coming until we got close, and we gave them a jolt of surprise as we passed no more than two feet overhead.

Most jeeps were equipped with radios that had antennas extending about seven feet high. We knew we were low enough when we heard the tick of the antenna hit the bottom of our helicopter. Our reputation preceded us. Whenever a vehicle's occupants heard or saw us flying low level, they scrambled to lower their antenna and duck down in the seat. I don't know what the guys on the ground thought, but we thought it was pure fun.

Tanks in our area were also considered a target. Their antennas extended about ten feet. After one successful tank-antenna strike, we shut down at Cam Lo, a marine firebase along Highway 9. A tank that was part of a convoy rumbled close to us and came to a halt. It leveled its 90-millimeter gun straight at me while I sat in the left seat of the cockpit, so I was now looking into the muzzle of a barrel only twenty-five feet away. An older, tough-looking marine got out of the turret and quickstepped up to my open door where I was eating a can of C-rations. He got right in my face. In his hand were pieces of a broken, three-quarter-inch, flat-ribbon antenna.

"Are you the wise guy that broke my antenna?" he demanded. "A helicopter with a black cat just like this one broke my antenna four hours ago."

He didn't give me a chance to answer before he went on. "Do you realize how you put us in danger since I could not communicate?" He was plenty mad and ready to take on all four of us.

"Gunny, I am sure sorry. I didn't think that thing would break, just bend a little," I said. I always referred to older enlisted marines as gunnies out of respect. We called older army sergeants "top" or "top sergeant" to show respect. "Gunny, you usually see us coming and put your antenna down."

"Well, by gosh, I didn't see you coming."

I knew right then that I had not only broken his antenna—even though I'm sure he could find a spare—but I had also hurt his pride. We had probably made him look bad in front of his men.

"It won't happen again," I said. "All I have is a couple of cases of C-rations and a container of fresh water, but you are welcome to them."

He didn't answer but kept mumbling about me being a "smart-aleck army kid pilot" as he walked back to his tank. For the remainder of my tour, I hit a few jeep antennas but never a tank again.

About twice each week between missions, we had a desire for extra excitement. Sometimes stupidity overtook our common sense. Once, while unloading supplies at Alpha 2 outpost on the DMZ, one of my FAC buddies, Cat Killer 2-2, Lieutenant O'Shields, said, "Hey 2-1, there is an NVA flag flying about five klicks north of here. I am calling in artillery trying to hit it."

"Tell artillery to cease fire," I said. "Give me a heading, and we'll get the dang thing."

Staying low level, we took up a heading of three hundred degrees as directed by O'Shields. After about two minutes, we could see the flag, a crimson banner with a gold star in the middle, flying in a stiff wind atop a forty-foot pole. Crossing over the DMZ was spooky. As the Ben Hai River, which is in the middle of the DMZ, passed by underneath us, I saw nothing but bomb craters. The river was wider than I thought.

A minute farther in, I started feeling uneasy because the terrain changed from complete desolation to some vegetation where the enemy could be in concealed positions. I felt like we were flying into an ambush. There were bound to be enemy patrols, as well as forward observers in the area.

Within another minute, we were hovering right next to the flag. The crew chief had trouble reaching the prize souvenir as it flopped around in our rotor wash. The wind made for an unstable hover. What first appeared to be a big adventure to tell our grandkids was turning against us fast.

"I don't think this thing will come off. It's wired to a pipe."

At that instant, I started hearing automatic weapons. I didn't see any flashes, but the sound was close and quickly grew in intensity. The enemy was probably shooting from well-camou-flaged bunkers.

"Let's get out of here," I said over the intercom, followed by, "Return fire."

We stayed low level at full power and flew back close to the same route we had flown in until we crossed the Ben Hai River back into South Vietnam.

I didn't tell the crew, but if we had been shot down and lost in North Vietnam, my tombstone would have read: *His name was Ford but was permanently changed to Dumb Butt while trying to get a flag in North Vietnam.* Since we often couldn't avoid the enemy, I decided never to intentionally try such a dumb stunt again.

Weather was one of our main obstacles. We never had formal weather briefings but flew by experience and reports from other pilots in the area. We never refused a mission or aborted due to the weather; we simply adjusted to whatever conditions we encountered. A few times, we were caught in terrific winds.

Once, while returning from a mission back to Hue at fifteen hundred feet, the weather deteriorated fast and forced us to low level. I was over Highway 1 flying south toward Hue and encountered a tailwind of more than fifty knots. I flew fifteen feet above the ground at about 100 to 110 knots indicated air speed. Even though the wind buffeted us around considerably, it was worth the thrill of flying at a ground speed estimated at two hundred miles per hour. Twice, the tail wind suddenly increased even more and lifted the horizontal stabilizer and our entire tail section. I was looking almost straight down even though the cyclic was pulled fully back between my legs. Man, that was fun. I remember the town, My Chanh, passing under us in a blur. I got to experience that only once.

I decided to stop at Hue to ride out the storm. I had a hard time hovering, so I stayed close to the landing strip and headed the nose of the helicopter into the wind as the door gunners slid the doors shut. I tried to put it on the ground, but the aircraft wanted to stay airborne. After finally getting firmly on the ground and keeping it at full RPM with slightly forward cyclic, we saw as high as seventy knots on the air speed indicator. Within fifty minutes, the wind subsided enough for us to head back to Da Nang. We found out later that we had flown in a typhoon.

Back at Da Nang after shutdown procedures were concluded, I was asked to report to our new commanding officer, Major Moore.

"Lieutenant Ford, battalion headquarters needs a staff officer," he said. "You would be outstanding to fill the position with your experience, extensive combat time, and your college management degree."

I stopped paying attention to Major Moore's remaining two to three minutes of persuasive conversation and waited for him to quit talking. I finally heard him say, "Well, Lieutenant, what do you think?"

I delayed my response on purpose and a few seconds later, I replied, "Sir, say again all after battalion staff duty." I was sure he was not about to repeat his speech again. That was my way of completely rejecting the offer. The way I saw it, there was nothing to consider.

"I was told you wouldn't take it." He looked at me. "There are plenty of officers who would want to quit flying and fill these career-advancement positions."

With a salute, I replied, "Yes, sir," and went to find some chow.

A sturdy marine lieutenant called out my name and intercepted me on the tarmac. It was Doug Frantz. I had competed against him in high school baseball, and we had become friends at the University of Oklahoma.

"My gosh, Doug," I said. "I didn't know you were over here."

He told me that he had gone to Platoon Leadership Class and received his commission when he graduated from OU. He'd been in country a month, hadn't seen action yet, and was stationed on the east side of the Marble Mountain runway that we shared with the marines. I asked him with a smile if he would like to be my door gunner for the day. He quickly declined. After some general conversation about what was happening back home, he asked me what it would take to survive a year in 'Nam.

"Get rid of that thing," I said, looking at his Colt 45 pistol. "Doug, I've medevaced a lot of lieutenants. That sidearm lets the enemy know you're an officer. Hide it and carry an M16."

Doug was the only person I saw during my tour that I had known in the States. He was lucky to survive a serious wound in Vietnam. He was honorably discharged, became an outstanding citizen, and lives in Enid, Oklahoma.

–21–

NVA POWS

Did I tell you about getting those two AK-47s as shown on the front of Life magazine, February 16, 1968? I was lucky—in more ways than one.

==================== 12 APR 68 Letter to Diane

We had been flying for an operation between Quang Tri and Dong Ha, bringing back supplies after medevacing two ARVN soldiers who must have been sick. Neither one had apparent wounds. On our way back, I started to call that we were two minutes out when I saw two soldiers walking by themselves in open territory. We slightly diverted our route to take a closer look.

The men appeared unarmed. A strong south wind was at their backs, and they looked to be trying to make their way back to North Vietnam. They wore ragtag khaki pants and shirts. We frequently saw this kind of uniform on the NVA. Whenever we saw suspected enemy in the wrong location, we shot them. We had no time to ask questions. I decided not to shoot these guys though. I wanted to take the time to find out for sure if they were the enemy.

We called the American advisor on the ground and asked if he had troops in the area where these two were walking. I described the location, and the advisor said, "Wait one."

He got back within thirty seconds. "My counterpart [a Vietnamese officer he was assigned to advise] wants you to kill them."

We flew over the two soldiers. I decided not to kill these unarmed guys out in the open. I told the door gunner to fire close to them to get their reaction. We were at two hundred feet when he shot about ten rounds within twenty meters of them. They hardly flinched, did not look up, and kept walking with the wind.

I was sure these were hardcore enemy soldiers. I called back to the operation and said, "How about giving me four soldiers, and we'll take these guys alive."

We had never captured anyone, but the situation seemed set up to make it happen. I needed extra soldiers to secure the two men if we expected our door gunners to continue to provide cover fire for us. The American on the ground said that he approved and would have extra soldiers ready.

We landed to pick up the ARVN soldiers, and the major got on our aircraft along with them. I had seen him several times in the last couple of months. He was a real go-getter, easy to talk to, and about five feet six. He moved like a 150-pound competitive wrestler.

On the way out to the two enemy soldiers, I distinctly remembered that all we had ever done every day was shoot the enemy. This time, I felt we were doing the right thing.

They had traveled over a klick while we had gone to pick up the major and soldiers. We flew right to them and planned to land within thirty feet of their location, knowing that our troops would jump out on either side and easily capture them. As soon as our skids touched the ground with the helicopter facing them, our worst nightmare occurred. Both of the soldiers had AK-47s that we had not seen from the air.

My copilot, Ken Riley, and I were fifteen meters from their muzzles when they started firing.

"Kill 'em! Kill 'em!" I yelled.

A small puff of smoke came from the AK on the left, which was pointed straight at me. The smoke lingered for a moment. Then another puff of smoke came slowly out of his barrel and stayed suspended in a circle around his weapon. All my senses had shut down. I think I heard myself yell "kill 'em" again. Everything had stopped.

Then I heard a deafening explosion. The major had jumped out on the left side and fired his M16 with the muzzle six inches from my ear. He fired at least seven rounds on semi-automatic at the enemy soldiers and killed the one in front of me. The other enemy combatant had fired five to six rounds before my gunner shot him in the legs as he ran. We discovered later the soldier had run out of ammunition. Our machine gunners had not been able to shoot when we landed because their M60s had stops that keep them from firing directly toward the front of the aircraft.

The major approached the soldier he had shot and confirmed him dead. The four ARVN soldiers exited our aircraft and approached the wounded enemy who was now on his knees with his arms up to surrender. One of the four ARVN soldiers put the muzzle of his rifle six inches in front of the enemy's chest and fired three rounds into it. The ARVN soldiers casually walked back and got on board. The major searched the enemy soldiers and took their weapons.

After we returned, the major climbed out, got my attention, and wanted to talk. The crew chief opened my door as I rolled the throttle back to flight idle and removed my helmet.

"Well, sir, we tried to take them alive," I said. "Thanks for your help. You saved our tail."

The major ejected a live cartridge out of the AK-47 of the soldier he had shot, and then he handed the live round and the AK to me. Five more live rounds were in the clip. He then gave me an empty casing he had picked up off the ground. I still have both cartridges.

Recently I found out that the head stamp on the base of the expended cartridge was a late World War II Russian reload. The live cartridge was made in North Korea in the early 1950s. I attempted to send the AK-47 home by way of a Merchant Marine, but it never made it.

The major was proud that he had saved my men and me from possible death. With a firm handshake, I told him, "Thanks again, sir. Hard to believe those two wanted to take us on, but I guess it was a better option than being captured. Someday if I have kids, they'll sure appreciate you. Let's get home so we can make babies."

He was brave and had quick-as-a-cat reactions. I can still see his athletic, confident grin.

I put my helmet back on as I wrapped in full RPM to take off. Before pulling pitch, we stayed in place until we got the major's attention. We all gave him a crisp salute.

–22–

EASTER CEASE-FIRE

I will be home sometime in late July. I am trying not to think about it because I don't want to start flying my missions any differently than before. I feel that what I've been through is more than most. If the VC or NVA haven't got me yet, they won't. Besides, by flying missions like I normally and should do, I teach new pilots much more than if I were overly cautious. So much happens every day—actually bad to write about. We lost a new pilot recently, W-1 Joe Reichlin, from Amherst, New York. He was very well liked. I guess I am getting used to seeing all this.

————————————————— 13 JUN 68 Letter to Diane

When a mission appears routine and not remotely dangerous, you tend to let your guard down. That happened on Easter Sunday, April 14, 1968. A cease-fire had been declared throughout Vietnam for that meaningful day.

I was never aware of the day of the week. Sunday, Monday, Tuesday—they were all the same. However, I was always aware of the date when filling out the logbook, composing a report, or writing a letter. Easter, along with Christmas and Thanksgiving, was special, even in a war zone. Soldiers were aware of these holidays. I knew we were going to be one of very few aircraft in the sky on Easter Sunday.

We prepared to take passengers from the ARVN headquarters to various outposts. Before the passengers could get on, a Vietnamese soldier ran up to our aircraft and jumped upon the skid with a map in his hand. I knew what was coming: we were going to get vague instructions.

He pointed to an area generally to the northeast of Hue and told me to go there because they needed help. Even though it was a cease-fire, I asked about the enemy situation. In broken English, he said there was "no VC, no VC, family real bad you go." He told me when they heard us coming, they would pop smoke.

I assumed this wasn't an emergency but a sick or injured civilian related to a village chief or a high-ranking officer. This had happened in the past. Sometimes a whole family would jump aboard and even bring their pets.

We took off and flew at eighty knots and two hundred feet off the ground. Just for fun, I made a call over the emergency frequency. I quickly asked if there was any Cat Killer in the area and to "come up uniform." We knew they were not flying and of course received no response. I just wanted to break the silence.

It was a good time to have my usual two- to three-minute breakfast, so I told my pilot he had the aircraft. Using the P-38 can opener on my dog-tag chain, I opened a can of C-ration peanut butter (sometimes it was cheese) and scooped the stuff out with round, hard C-ration crackers.

Holidays were usually quiet. I recalled that in 1914 during World War I, British and German soldiers at Christmas got out of their fox-holes, sang Christmas carols, played soccer together, and some even exchanged gifts.

The Huey felt so smooth it seemed to be on autopilot. We rarely flew at this leisurely altitude and speed. I was enjoying it and mentioned it to the crew. I flew by resting two fingers on top of the cyclic. Then out of the quiet and calm, things changed in an instant as a burst of automatic weapons fired off to our right-rear side, and I felt two ticks hit the helicopter.

I instantly switched to combat mode. In five seconds, I had cross-checked for warning lights, determined that there was no serious damage to the aircraft, and confirmed that no one on board had been shot. I noted the terrain the fire had come from and the type of weapons used. In those five seconds, my mind was made up. I decided to engage them as I made a hard-right descending turn. The door gunner returned fire without hesitation, and I said over the intercom, "We are going back. Keep firing."

I don't know which made me madder, letting my guard down or these guys trying to kill us during a cease-fire. My door gunner did his job. He never stopped firing. He told me later that the muzzle flashes gave him an easy target as we closed in. He killed one immediately and another two as they ran for cover—probably they had run out of ammo or did not think we would come back for them.

I was still looking for a fight. We hovered while making a 360-degree pedal turn as the door gunners fired into suspected enemy locations.

"Good job," I told the gunners. "Way to nail 'em—even if it is Easter."

We continued the mission and found the family that needed help. One of the village leaders had been assassinated. We loaded him and his family and did not take any chances on our return, flying right on the deck at one hundred knots all the way back to Hue.

I couldn't get over being angry. The entire country was under a declared cease-fire, and the guys who fired at us had ignored it or had not been informed. We were easy targets and could have been the only casualties in the war on Easter Sunday.

My next passengers hopped on. On our way north, I thought of something that would ease my mind and calm me down. We climbed to twenty-five hundred feet to make sure my transmission could be picked up by distant locations. I switched to the emergency frequency and distinctly broadcast, "Any station, any station, this is Black Cat 2-1 on guard. Negative cease-fire in Vietnam—out."

Over the intercom, I said, "How about that?"

The crew appreciated it, and I had to laugh at my own cleverness. It sure made me feel better. The remainder of the day passed without incident.

Apparently bases of operation and some other aircraft picked up my transmission. I was surprised by how many asked about it over the next few weeks.

−23−

THE NUNG

The missions we fly put us right in the middle of the enemy every day. It is a shame so many great young men don't make it home. I can feel proud that I've made it this far and am this close to coming home.

— 05 JUL 68 Letter to Mom, Dad, and Bill

During my last four months in country, rocket and mortar attacks were a regular occurrence. Mortars were not as life threatening. We slept in a bunker that had three layers of sand bags and, although never tested, could take a direct hit. Our living quarters were surrounded by soft sand that could absorb the impact of a mortar and also muffle the sound. I actually slept through attacks with mortars landing within one hundred meters.

Rockets were another matter. The safest place during a rocket attack was in an eight-foot by eight-foot by ten-foot steel Conex container that the construction battalion of the Navy Seabees had buried ten feet underground. The Seabees had a reputation—they could do anything and get it done fast. There was an opening cut for a ladder, and when rocket attacks became more frequent, they built wooden bunk beds in the Conex. Even when the all-clear sounded, we were usually too tired to climb out and so slept there until morning. There wasn't extra bedding available, so we slept on the bunk boards and used rolled-up jungle fatigues for pillows. It wasn't too difficult to get used to sleeping like that knowing you were safe.

During my last two months in country, even though the missions were challenging, they became routine. Contact with the enemy and flying in and out of hot LZs was normal. I knew from experience that if I kept my crew informed and made sure they were ready, they would do their job every minute.

Two missions during this time were memorable. The first was a resupply on the side of a mountain. When I asked the troops to pop smoke at two minutes out, two different colors of smoke rose from the mountainside about one klick apart. This had happened before, so I chose one and said, "I've got yellow smoke."

With obvious panic, the guy on the ground said, "Negative, negative, that's not us."

"Roger negative yellow. I have purple in sight," I said.

After we heard "Roger purple," I told the crew to make note of the yellow smoke. We would engage those guys later.

I flew close to the side of the mountain and encountered terrific downdraft conditions. As we eased into the opening, the main rotor blade was only two feet from the mountainside directly in front of us. It was so steep that we were still not close enough to hand the supplies to the men, and they were not prepared for us to toss the supplies to them. The strong downdraft and delay with a fully loaded Huey made me realize we would soon run out of power. The low-RPM audio began screaming as the aircraft started to settle.

"Breaking right at this time," I transmitted and dove down the side of the mountain. The main-rotor RPM rose nicely and gave me time to come up with a better plan.

I called the guys on the ground. "Get more troops in the LZ. Be prepared. I'm coming back. We have to drop everything to you. I will get as close as I can."

When we got back to the LZ, they were ready. As soon as we eased into position, our door gunners dropped the supplies out to troops waiting three to five feet below the skids—too far to hand them. They caught most of the supplies. Only a few things fell through their hands and crashed down the mountainside.

One soldier decided to carry a box of C-rations under each arm up the side of the mountain toward our main rotor. The higher he went, the closer he got. Our main rotor blade was now within a foot of the mountain. He kept his head down as he climbed within inches. I saw him just in time and slightly jerked the cyclic up and to the right. The helicopter rose about one foot, barely avoiding slicing into the soldier's skull, and we flew down the mountainside.

We picked up more supplies and returned with much needed batteries, which were always in short supply. My gunners had a good idea. They tied WD-1 communications wire around the batteries and lowered each to the soldiers on the ground.

With the mission accomplished, we broke away from the mountain and told the American advisor we were going to the area where we had seen the yellow smoke. He confirmed, so we then expended half of our ammo on the suspected enemy location. The American advisor appreciated our extra fire support.

With forty-five days left in country, I volunteered for a mission to fly in support of the special forces. The briefing for the mission was at 4:30 a.m. at FOB-1, the farthest-north forward operating base, which was close to Phu Bai. We took off from Da Nang for the forty-minute flight at three thirty, refueled hot at Phu Bai airfield, and flew the short distance to the base. There were four other Hueys waiting, two each from the 101st Airborne and the First Cavalry. For cover support, we had two newly arrived Cobra gunships.

The briefing was typical special forces. We walked into a small room with an officer standing beside a red curtain with block letters that read, "Top Secret." I thought to myself, *I don't want to see what's on the other side of that curtain. Just tell us where they are, and we'll go get them.* But that's not how special forces operated. They always threw the worst-case scenario at you.

The officer slid back the curtain. He wore a Ranger tab, a small patch on his left shoulder, which usually indicated a West Point graduate.

"Gentlemen, here is the situation," he began. "We have men surrounded." He pointed to a mountaintop in eastern Laos at an elevation of approximately twenty-seven hundred feet. "They must be extracted before daylight. Four Vietnamese H-34s attempted extraction last night and aborted after one was shot down on final approach for pickup. Take off all identification. If you go down, you will be listed as missing in action for the duration."

I knew that meant duration of the war and probably forever. Laos was unauthorized territory for US personnel. The special forces officer quickly pointed out on the map all the enemy locations that surrounded the pinnacle LZ, and he said it had been reported they had .51-caliber capability. That got our attention.

He asked for any questions but there weren't any. We were ready to go.

We took off forty-five seconds apart in trail formation. We designated ourselves as Chalk 1 through 5, and I was Chalk 4. An air force forward air controller with the call sign Covey flew above to help if needed. There was room for only one Huey in the LZ. En route, I repeated to the crew what I'd heard in the briefing.

"Make sure you have a fresh can of ammo and clear your weapons," I added. "Any questions?" No one answered, so I asked them again, "Are you ready? Clear your weapons."

Still no one would answer. I wanted to get them to talk. "OK guys, say this after me—row, row, row your boat. I start, and you join in."

It took three times before I finally got a weak "gently down the stream" from one of them. They cleared their M60s. We were getting close.

Chalk 1 was on final descent from fifteen hundred feet above the LZ. I could see a hand-held strobe light on top of the mountain and muzzle flashes from three sides below. When the troops were on board, Chalk 1 transmitted, "Coming out." The Cobras timed their run to cover the exit as Chalk 2 was on final approach. Every landing and takeoff was coordinated beautifully.

I made a fast approach and zeroed our ground speed as the skids lightly touched down. The cockpit extended off the edge of the mountaintop. We could see a blanket of gunfire when looking down through the clear Plexiglas chin bubble. We were there for less than ten seconds when my crew chief said, "They're on."

"Chalk 4 coming out," I transmitted. The Cobras timed their gun run as I was pulling pitch to exit the tiny LZ. Both our gunners fired straight down to cover our exit as we climbed to altitude.

When we were two minutes from landing back at the forward operating base, we received a call from the forward air controller.

Covey broadcasted, "All Chalk aircraft, be advised some were left in the LZ. Who has enough fuel to go back?"

In thirty seconds, we were on short final, and no one had volunteered. I'm sure the other four were calculating their fuel requirement. I checked our fuel indicator, which read about seven hundred pounds. We were good.

"What do you think about going back?" I asked the crew.

They didn't answer. I made up my mind.

I transmitted, "Covey, this is Chalk 4. As soon as my PAX offload, we'll go."

Now we were a flight of one, but I had two Cobras that were going to be by our side. On the way, I asked if everyone was ready. There was no answer.

I had been in their position many times. Going back to a hot LZ was always more difficult. You feel like your luck will run out. The fear of death overwhelms your senses, and talking becomes much harder. I told the gunners to clear their weapons. When we were halfway back, I still had not received a response. I tried three times.

"OK, girls," I finally said over the intercom. "This is no time to throw our dresses over our heads and go home. We have to go get these guys."

I was just as scared as they were, but experience kicked in. I knew if I acted brave, no one would know the difference. I had used this "dress-over-the-head" line before in tight spots with the crew. It worked. Without answering, they both cleared their weapons and gave two affirmative clicks over the intercom.

One gunner softly said, "We're with you, sir."

Sure made me proud.

My copilot, W-1 Culp, had not spoken the entire mission. He had been in country about two months. This was his first time to fly with me.

Pulling the last guys out of this location was going to take perfect timing. The NVA would be ready for us.

As we approached the pinnacle, I saw the partially burned wreckage of the H-34 from the previous night's attempted extraction. Enormous enemy gunfire erupted. The Cobras dove at the gunfire and delivered fire to cover our approach. On short final, I said over the intercom to my copilot, "Culp, do you want to land this one?" I glanced at him and saw only bulging eyes of disbelief. It brought a quick, private chuckle. "Stay close."

We touched down and looked at the gunfire through the chin bubble. There was much more than the first time. A few green tracers zipped by us and appeared to gain speed as they passed. I knew that it would be impossible to fly through it this time. In that moment, I felt completely alone.

Our door gunner said, "There is only one and he is on."

We had to go. "Chalk 4 coming out," I transmitted.

As I pulled in full power and nosed the Huey down for takeoff, I thought, *This is it. There is no way we will make it.*

At that instant, one of the Cobras came from above and dove straight down in front of us toward the enemy gunfire, all of his weapons firing. His skids passed no more than two feet from my main rotor blade. I flinched, but then I knew: *We have a chance.*

His wingman followed him slightly to our right, his weapons blasting into the enemy positions. The Cobras took on the entire enemy force face to face. I climbed out and leveled off at three thousand feet. We had won, and it was a magnificent sight.

The faster Cobras, much lighter now, circled us twice, banking ninety degrees in front of us in what we took as victory laps. What a sight. I said over the intercom, "The most lethal weapon in warfare ever invented has to be a fully armed Cobra in the hands of a twenty-year-old warrant officer aviator."

My gosh, those guys were good.

I told the gunners, "Way to go. Good job," and added, "Hey, Culp, you would have come through if I needed you." He didn't answer, so I looked at him and got a smile.

Not much was said on the way back. Total relief never occurred until we were back on the ground in a secure area.

By the time we returned to the base, it was full light. I glanced back to see who we had picked up and saw one soldier.

"Who is that?" I asked.

The red-and-blue scarf he wore threw me. After all that, had we picked up an NVA soldier? I took his picture.

The last special forces soldier was a Nung, one of the ethnic Chinese living in Vietnam and often employed as mercenaries. They were excellent fighters trained in reconnaissance and were led by our special forces to conduct cross-border operations into Laos. The US public was told that American soldiers never crossed the border—regardless of the reason. When we volunteered, all of us knew that was why the mission was top secret.

The special forces had breakfast ready for us. They returned our dog tags and other identification. I noticed all the other pilots were warrants.

During breakfast, the lighthearted conversation turned to discussion of how close we were to our DEROS. When I told them my DEROS was forty-five days, I was greeted with an almost-hostile disbelief. Some thought that any pilot who was close to going home would not have his mind 100 percent on the mission and would jeopardize everyone. It was hardly believable to them that anybody that short would volunteer for such a mission. The closest to my DEROS was one pilot with five months left in country.

I stood up to give them my answer.

"First of all, I never thought about being short until you guys brought it up," I started. "It's always rewarding to fly for the special forces because you get an 'attaboy' medal and a good breakfast, and we all got both this morning."

Two or three pilots realized my attempt at humor and said, "He's right."

I looked directly at the Cobra guys and said, "Good job. We never would have made it without you." They acted as if they were still wired up and ready to reload and go back again.

The pilots were almost satisfied with my answer. A few said they still thought I was *beaucoup dinkidou*, Vietnamese slang for big-time crazy, but they said it with a smile.

We refueled and flew missions for the rest of the day, getting in late once again. It was another rewarding day. The warrant officers made an impression on me, and I decided they had a reasonable point. I did not volunteer to fly any more top secret missions.

—24—

LAST 40 DAYS

I feel I've done my job and accomplished every mission, and now I'm ready to come home. I really can't see how a helicopter pilot could last any more than one year.

===================== 15 JUL 68 Letter to Diane*

With forty days left in country, I wanted to stay busy and continue to fly in my northern AO. I had a feeling that when I got close to my DEROS, I would acquire the much-talked-about short-timer's syndrome and finish flying. It's said that when you get it, you will know it. A pilot will think more about surviving and going home than about his mission. I set a goal to keep my mind combat-ready and not let anyone down. Soon I knew I would wake up with one week left in country. At that time, I promised myself to check in my flight gear.

I planned out my last week in country, which included sleeping in every day, hanging out in the sun, and reading *The Carpetbaggers* by Harold Robbins. McKinsey had it beside the tape recording he had made for me of The Mamas & the Papas. I had seen Mac read it when our two ships occasionally ended up together in a secure LZ for a C-ration lunch.

I took a mission to the Hoi An area and all points south. I had not been that direction since the previous August when Bart Colburn and I flew as two copilots on a CA. I thought a change would be

---

*Written five days before leaving Vietnam.

215

good and make the time go faster. Taking off from Marble Mountain, slowly climbing to altitude, and heading south reminded me of flight school. Every location we resupplied lacked the intensity of those in the northern I Corps area. I felt guilty all day that I was not flying in my normal AO, knowing I was depended upon. Hearing the soldiers on the ground say, "Is that you, 2-1?" and "Good," after I called them when five minutes from their location, was an acknowledgment of my reputation. It was a solid satisfaction that recognition of combat produces in a pilot. I was glad when the day was over and I could return to my regular AO. I did not go back.

Walking close to the platoon hootch, a staff officer from battalion headquarters approached and called me by name. As he returned my salute, I thought, *Whatever he wants can't be good.*

He quickly got to the point and asked if I would be willing to leave Vietnam in four days and join a group that would tour America. The group would speak on behalf of the army in general and specifically about the mission of the military in Vietnam. There had been a request for a helicopter pilot with combat experience. We would give a presentation three times a week to different organizations like Rotary and Kiwanis clubs and the VFW.

Leaving thirty days before my tour was finished was not acceptable. I was doing so much every day. I was maintaining a high skill level and knew it; the Huey did everything I wanted it to do, practically by thinking it. I looked forward to each mission and going beyond what was expected of me. The thought of telling anyone I came home thirty days before my original DEROS—well, I could not even imagine it.

I got a sick feeling that I might be ordered to go home and quickly thought, *Somehow you gotta talk your way out of this.* Thankfully the major asked if I would think it over and report to him by 9:00 a.m.

with my answer, but I did not need that much time. I saluted him and gave him an immediate terse response.

"Sir, I cannot leave before my tour is finished." I held the salute. "Thank you for considering me, but no thanks, sir."

I continued to hold my salute, and he knew further conversation was unnecessary. Hesitantly he returned my salute, nodded, and said, "OK." He walked away.

With three weeks left in country, our new commanding officer, Major Garrett, asked if I would represent the 282nd and serve on a court martial board during morning hours for the next two days. He said the board needed experienced guys like me. I remembered testifying on behalf of Payne and thought I could do some good as a member of the board.

"Yes, sir. It would be an honor."

Being on the five-member court martial board was a good experience. The other four staff officers were solid men of higher rank who encouraged me to ask questions and listened to my suggestions for punishment. It was not difficult to determine proper penalties, if any. If the accused conducted himself like a soldier, that was how we treated him. Bad conduct and attitudes were dealt with accordingly.

To fill the time at night, I played ping-pong, pickup basketball games, and twenty-five-cent maximum-bet poker games with the longer-in-country pilots, which were full of laughs. One night, I watched ten minutes of a lousy movie at the company theater. I wrote a few letters home.

With thirty days left, I flew north almost every day, not thinking about the end of my tour. It never crossed my mind to be cautious. I had a strong desire to pass on what I'd learned and teach new pilots by example what it took to be successful and stay alive.

Instead of flying with a new peter pilot on lightning bug missions, each time I asked an AC from the gun platoon such as W-2 Dick Crosby or W-2 Jim Burnett to go with me. ACs in the guns always flew in the right seat, and this gave me security.

With only two weeks left in country, I flew one night with Burnett in the right seat. The air was smooth, and there had been no enemy contact. I was totally relaxed, so much so that I fell into a deep sleep. An hour passed before Burnett said over the intercom, "Hey, Bob, we are low on fuel. Let's go home. Do you want to fly it back?"

Suddenly awake, I didn't know where I was. I handled the controls, but everything felt foreign. I had no idea what was happening.

"Jim, I can't wake up," I said. "You better fly it back."

At first, he thought I was kidding. He laughed at me all the way back while I tried to shake the cobwebs out of my mind. During shutdown, he never quit chuckling and asked if I wanted him to stick around and tuck me into my bunk. I knew my combat flying was coming to an end. I had no business flying any serious missions during my last two weeks.

With one week left in country, the word came through the channels that I was going to be promoted to captain. During wartime, promotions get accelerated. Our platoon leader, Captain Zeltner, came to me with the signed captain orders in hand, but instead of handing them to me, he held them up above his shoulder and said, "Before you are promoted, there will be an official ceremony at the officers' club tonight."

With several other pilots joining us around a table that night, Captain Zeltner poured three inches of Scotch whiskey in a glass, dropped in the captain's bars, and said, "Lieutenant Ford, when those railroad tracks are firmly in your teeth, you will officially be promoted to captain."

For someone who drank only an occasional beer, this was going to be a challenge.

Things soon got fuzzy, but I finally secured the captain's bars to a few shouts and applause. The same bell I had polished almost a year ago clanged. As tradition dictated, I bought a round for everyone in the club. The tab was about thirty dollars, but the older warrants were looking after me. They escorted me to the high-stakes poker game and stood behind me to make sure I won about fifty dollars. All the players were in on it. I paid the thirty-dollar bar tab.

Everything was spinning as I started for my hootch. Just then, the incoming warning siren sounded. Within seconds, mortars began impacting our area. The whiskey was still affecting my judgment, and I stayed out in the open, walking throughout the compound area and yelling highly colorful words at the enemy. I told them they'd had all year to kill me and hadn't gotten me yet. I reasoned the safest place in South Vietnam was right next to me. Of course, nobody else thought so because no one was willing to join me out in the open.

Occasionally I heard a muffled voice from inside a bunker say, "Ford, dang it, get in here."

But that only contributed to my rant. I yelled, "Get out of your bunker. The safest place in South Vietnam is right by me."

And so it went until the all clear sounded.

About noon the next day, I bought a Vietnamese-made olive drab hat that had white captain's bars and aviator wings stitched on the front. I kept my promise to quit flying and checked in my flight gear. I told the supply sergeant I had orders to be an instructor pilot at Fort Wolters, and I would like to keep my flight helmet. It had become a part of me. Like the jungle fatigues I got from the First Cavalry infantry captain when I first arrived in country, I felt this helmet helped get me through my tour.

He told me to come back the next day, and he would see what he could do. The sarge did some kind of battle-damage paper shuffle, and the next day gave me my helmet. I still have it. I saluted him first and said, "Thanks, Sarge."

"Glad to do it, Captain—you earned it."

I knew he meant it, and "Captain" sounded good to me. We shook hands.

The day was here. I was going home. I needed a jeep ride to the Da Nang main air facility to catch my C-130 flight to Cam Rahn Bay for out-processing. Suddenly the warning system sounded—there were incoming mortars. This was a rare daytime attack. Everyone scrambled for a bunker except for one new aircraft commander.

"Hey 2-1," he yelled at me. "I'll get you out of here."

He stopped a crew chief running by and told him, "Go untie your aircraft. We're getting Captain Ford out of here. He's earned the right to go home!"

He told the crew chief to get in the right seat and then hollered, "Get on board, sir."

I sure liked this kid. He was the type who was ready to do any-thing. He would have been a perfect fit with my guys during our time at Hue. He got me to Da Nang in good shape, and I got in line to board the C-130. There was one day left on my DEROS.

The next day, we were "leavin' on a jet plane"—a civilian 707. We were going to cross the big pond and go home. When we landed at Fort Lewis, Washington, I heard a mild clapping when the wheels touched down. It was hard to believe I'd made it.

I asked myself if I had changed. I had seen movies in which those who had experienced combat could not cope with civilian life. Would I have problems adjusting? I told myself I wouldn't and thought of all my plans and goals. I imagined my homecoming with a loving wife, brother, sisters, mom, and dad; getting back into shape; being the best instructor pilot in the army; starting a career in the family business; and having children who looked up to and loved their father. All of these thoughts started spinning through my mind as soon as I hit American soil.

I had faced intense combat and knew I would be proud for the rest of my life that I came through many tough experiences. During my tour, I realized that what was happening back home was not as important as completing every mission and taking care of my crew. We did not take the time to talk about war protesters, draft dodgers, or those who chose to high tail it to Canada, and even the assassinations of Reverend King and Bobby Kennedy were hardly discussed.

I had experienced a part of history and flying at its most satisfying and thrilling—being single ship, given a radio frequency and location of ground troops, then trusting the teamwork of my entire crew to take care of any situation no matter the enemy condition or weather. I knew the Black Cat call sign, like our gunships the Alley Cats, would always be one of respect and honor.

I had done my duty and what was expected of me. I had served with honor and dedication to our country as an army combat helicopter pilot with America's best.

I feel certain that when the Hue detachment warrant officer pilots, crew chiefs, and door gunners read this, they'll say, "Well, Boss, you did it. You wrote it. You did a good job—for a lieutenant."

My answer:

I'd do it all again with you guys, and I'd do it for free.

–Epilogue–

OKEENE, OKLAHOMA

I requested and received orders for Fort Wolters, Texas. I was going to be an instructor pilot back where it all began for me. This was the beginning of the best year of my life. I really couldn't believe I had made it back alive. On top of that, every day I got to instruct warrant officer candidate pilots flying the TH-55 helicopter in contact training during their third and fourth month of flight school. I loved every minute of it.

My first child, Amy, was born in Beach Army Hospital at the Fort Wolters post in Mineral Wells on April 20, 1969. I was so glad to be alive, and having a child made my homecoming complete. I'd seen so much death and dying in Vietnam. Having a baby turned the focus to life and living.

My three-year obligation to the army was up on July 20, 1969. It had been a life-changing three years. We moved to Okeene, and I started working on July 28 for the Shawnee Milling Company. My dad wanted me to learn the milling business there and then come back to Shawnee in a few years. But I liked being on my own, running the flour mill in Okeene. It was the challenge I needed then, and it's still challenging every day. It's rewarding to work with my brother, Bill, and his son, Joe, who run the operations in Shawnee. We have a solid, successful team to carry on the family business.

I love Okeene. Everybody in town from six to one hundred knows me by my first name. Diane and I had two more children, Allison and Tyler, who were born in 1972 and 1980. I've been able to enjoy school, community, and church activities in Okeene and have filled a leadership role in each. I played every sport available—tennis, racquetball, basketball, and softball. Everywhere I went, at least one of my great kids was in my hip pocket. I coached little-league football, boys' basketball, and girls' softball. I've enjoyed hunting, fishing, and raising cattle, as well as growing wheat and canola.

Every year, I organize the Veterans Day program in Okeene. I wear the uniforms I wore flying in combat, as well as my dress greens to honor all veterans. I speak to the high school juniors and seniors at 8:00 a.m. and then spend a rewarding hour and a half with the third graders. Before I finish, one of the little girls gets to put on my flight helmet and jacket. When I slide the tinted visor down on the helmet, all the kids burst into laughter. At 11:00 a.m., I introduce the year's guest speaker in the high school auditorium, and the entire town is invited. It's always a memorable and patriotic occasion.

As a tribute to the contribution the Huey made to saving lives in Vietnam, I located the shell of a 1965 Huey D Model in 2009. Ex-crew chief Jerry Staggs spent two years restoring it in Weatherford, Texas, with help from another former crew chief, Mike Peterson. The Huey was then transported and put on permanent display in Shawnee, Oklahoma, at Veterans Park next to the courthouse and the old Carnegie Library. I was honored to give the dedication speech on July 4, 2011. I'm proud the Huey is part of this majestic and honorable setting.

Keeping my wartime promise to stay in shape, I have competed in more than 250 races from 5Ks to marathons. The most rewarding have been the triathlons. I won the state championship of my age group in the short and long course ten separate years. I received all-American honors seven different times. I competed in two Ironman races that include a 2.4-mile swim, a 112-mile bike ride, and a 26.2-mile run—the first in eleven hours, seven minutes and the second in ten hours, fifty-seven minutes.

The guys I lost in Vietnam—and all of those we supported on the ground—are in my heart every day, especially Dedrick and McKinsey. In August 1992, while running the last mile of an Ironman in Santa Rosa, California, I had a vivid experience that involved them. During the last mile of the event, I strongly felt that I was in their presence. I knew that when I looked up, I would somehow see them—and I did.

There they were in front of me, their faces filling up half the sky as plain as any face I'd ever seen. They were talking between themselves and smiling. I heard them say that I should be proud for completing every mission in Vietnam and for finishing this race.

"Boss, you're doing great," they told me. I clearly heard them say, "Don't be in any hurry to get up here."

I continued toward the finish line and answered them with a heart full of gratitude. "Thanks for being here with me."

–Glossary–

TERM	MEANING
A-1 Skyraider	World War II-era, heavily armed, single-engine propeller aircraft with great staying power used often to protect downed pilots. Made by Douglas.
AC	Aircraft Commander, pilot in charge of aircraft.
ADF	Automatic Directional Finding radio. When a pilot tunes into a preset beacon frequency, a needle shows the direction of the beacon relative to the aircraft. Each beacon transmits its identifying call letters in Morse Code. Phu Bai was the only ADF in our AO.
Agent Orange	Toxic defoliant sprayed on vegetation to deny cover for the enemy.
Air Strike	Surface attack by fixed-wing/bomber aircraft.
AK-47	Automatic assault rifle that was the standard individual weapon of enemy troops.
Alley Cat	Call sign for heavily armed gunships with the 282nd Assault Helicopter Company. Flew Huey B models.
AO	Area of Operation, a defined geographical area where military missions are flown.
Article 15	Punishment under the Uniform Code of Military Justice. Less severe than a general court martial.
ARVN	Army of the Republic of Vietnam, South Vietnam, our allies.
Aussie	Australian Army Training Team-Vietnam.
Beaucoup	Pronounced "boo-ku," French for "large amount."
Betel Nut	Nut from the betel palm chewed like tobacco for its mild narcotic effect.
Bird Dog	Light, single-engine propeller aircraft made by Cessna used to direct artillery fire and air support, flown by forward air controllers in our AO. Call sign Cat Killer.
Black Cat	Call sign for the 282nd Assault Helicopter Company.

Blood Chit	A small object made of silk-like material, depicting the American flag and a statement in several languages (Chinese, Laotian, Vietnamese, Cambodian). Anyone assisting the bearer to safety was rewarded.
Body Bag	Bags constructed of plastic and canvas used to take American dead from battle areas.
Bunker	Defensive fortification designed to protect soldiers from rockets, mortars, and ground attacks.
C-130	Medium-range, four-engine, propeller-driven aircraft used for carrying cargo or as many as sixty soldiers.
CA	Combat Assault.
Cat Killer	See "Bird Dog."
Chalk	Term for position in a formation. Chalk 1 was the lead.
Collective	Collective pitch control is normally located on the left side of the pilot's seat. The collective changes the pitch angle of the main rotor blades collectively—both at the same time. If a collective input is made, the result is that the helicopter increases or decreases its total lift derived from the rotor. In level flight, this would cause a climb or descent or produce acceleration.
Colt 45	Model 1911 .45-caliber semiautomatic pistol. Standard-issue sidearm, held seven rounds.
CO	Commanding Officer. Officer in command of a company. Nickname: the Old Man.
C-ration	Canned individual meals opened with supplied can opener, called a P-38.
Crew Chief	Enlisted specialist, maintainer of aircraft. Manned one of the M60s on left side.
Cyclic	Cyclic control is usually located between the pilot's legs and is commonly called the cyclic stick. It is similar in appearance to a joystick in a conventional aircraft. It changes the angle of the rotor blades. Forward cyclic coordinated with increased power moves the helicopter forward—to hover, the cyclic is in a stationary/neutral position.

Daiwi	Captain in Vietnamese.
DEROS	Date Eligible Return from Overseas. Going home.
Deuce and a Half	A two-and-a-half-ton military transport truck capable of carrying 5,000 pounds.
Dinkidou	Crazy in Vietnamese.
DMZ	Demilitarized Zone that separated South Vietnam from North Vietnam.
Door Gunner	Crewman tasked with firing one and maintaining both M60s. Sat on right side.
E&E	Escape & Evasion from enemy.
ETA	Estimated Time of Arrival.
Extraction	The removal of troops from the battlefield.
F-4 Phantom	McDonnell Douglas fighter bomber, flew with a crew of one pilot and one weapons officer.
FAC	Forward Air Control.
Fast Movers	US fighter/bombers, jets.
Fire Base or Fire Support Base	Forward Artillery Base.
Firefight	Small-arms battle.
Fire Mission	Directed artillery barrage.
Firefly	Mounting a searchlight on a Huey to locate an enemy with gunship support.
Flak Vest	Vest worn by US soldiers to lessen the severity of torso wounds.
Flight Idle	Aircraft engine and rotor blades running at 55 percent of full throttle while stationary on the ground.
FOB	Forward Operating Base for special forces.
Free Fire Zone	An area declared off-limits to all personnel. Anyone encountered within its confines was assumed to be hostile and could be fired upon without verification or authorization.
Guard	Emergency frequency 121.5 VHF or 242 UHF.

Gunship	See Alley Cat.
H-34	Single-rotor cargo helicopter used by the ARVN and marines.
H-46	The Boeing H-46 Sea Knight, a medium-lift, tandem-rotor cargo helicopter used by the United States Marine Corps to provide transport of combat troops, supplies, and equipment to ground troops.
Hootch	Small civilian family or military shelter.
Hot	Term describing an AO or LZ where contact has been made with enemy troops.
HQ	Headquarters.
Hue	Imperial capital of Vietnam. Pronounced "Way."
Huey UH-1 Helicopter	Primary helicopter used in Vietnam.
I Corps	Northern-most military district of South Vietnam.
ID	Identify.
IFR	Instrument Flight Rules, flight by instruments. Used in flying conditions so poor you must rely on instruments.
In Country	In Vietnam.
Insertion	Placement of combat or reconnaissance forces in the field by helicopter.
IP	Instructor Pilot, a pilot with additional rating who trains other pilots.
JP-4	Jet Propellant fuel used in Army Huey turbine engines.
Jack Benny	Used Jack Benny's never-changing age, 39, to quickly advise FM ground frequency to other aircraft. Example: "Go Jack Benny plus 2.3" was 41.3.
KIA	Killed in Action.
Klick	1,000 meters, a kilometer, or .62 mile. 10 miles = 16 klicks.
Knots	Used as a unit of speed in a helicopter. 100 knots = 115 miles per hour.

KP	Kitchen Police, term for those assigned to work in the mess hall.
Landline or Lima Lima	Ground-telephone communication between two points.
Lightning Bug	See "Firefly."
LST	Landing Ship Tank, a naval vessel that supports landings on shore.
LT	Lieutenant.
LTC	Lieutenant Colonel.
LZ	Landing Zone for helicopters.
M1 Garand	.30-caliber WWII-era semiautomatic rifle.
M2	.30-caliber carbine, semi- or fully automatic.
M14	Fires the 7.62-mm NATO round (.30-caliber), semi- or fully automatic, used by marines until 1968.
M16	Lightweight automatic assault rifle. 5.56 mm (.22-caliber), became standard American weapon, semi- or fully automatic.
M60	7.62-mm NATO machine guns with thumb button trigger on the grips, used on helicopters. .30-caliber, fires about 550 rounds per minute.
M79	Shoulder-fired, single-shot, 40-mm grenade launcher.
MACV	Military Assistance Command Vietnam. Combined headquarters for all branches of the services in Vietnam.
Medevac	Helicopter conducting a medical evacuation.
Mermite Containers	General-purpose thermally insulated metal containers used to haul hot food or liquid to the troops in the field.
Mess	Food for soldiers. Served in mess hall.
MIA	Missing in Action.
Mini Gun	Mounted on both sides of Hueys and Cobra gunships, each has seven barrels that fire and rotate at high speed, capable of firing 6,000 rounds per minute or 100 rounds per second.
Monsoon	Rainy season in Southeast Asia.

MPC	Military payment certificate, paper worth 5 cents to $20. Script money issued to US military personnel.
Muzzle Flash	Bright flash of light produced at the end of the barrel of a rifle when fired.
NCO	Noncommissioned officer—sergeant—enlisted rank E-5 through E-9.
Number 1	Slang for the very best.
Number 10	Slang for the very worst.
Nung	An ethnic Chinese living in Vietnam, often employed as mercenaries.
NVA	North Vietnamese Army or a member of that army.
OD	Olive Drab, grayish olive to dark olive cloth used by the military.
OH	Observation Helicopter designed for observation missions or training.
Operations Officer	Assigns crews to aircraft for combat missions and assists in planning all missions.
PAX	Passengers.
Pedal Turn	While at a hover, a helicopter may rotate on its vertical axis using the antitorque pedals located at the pilot's feet.
Pedals, Tail Rotor	Also called antitorque pedals, the tail rotor pedals are located in the same position as the rudder pedals in an airplane and serve a similar purpose to control the direction in which the nose of the aircraft is pointed.
Peter Pilot	Copilot of a helicopter.
POL	Petroleum Oil and Lubrication. Refueling stations.
Posit	Known position or location.
POW	Prisoner of War.
PRC-25	Portable radio communication used by American combat troops.
PSP	Perforated Steel Plating or platform used for bunker construction, airstrip, bridge matting, or helicopter pads.
PT	Physical Training. Well-structured exercise.

Pulling Rank	Pulling rank is using your command position in giving orders or obtaining privileges.
Pull In Power	Term used by helicopter pilots that means they are taking off.
Pull Pitch	Same as "Pull in Power."
Push	Slang for radio frequency.
PX	Post Exchange, like a civilian department store.
R&R	Rest & Recuperation. Five- to seven-day out-of-country furloughs given to US military personnel serving in a combat zone.
Recon	Small unit that explores an area especially to gather military information in enemy territory.
ROTC	Reserve Officer Training Corps. Military training for college students leading to a commission as a second lieutenant upon graduation.
RPG	Shoulder-fired, rocket-propelled grenade launcher used by enemy, also "B40."
RPM	Revolutions per minute. Measure of circular speed.
Scud	Ragged, low clouds moving rapidly beneath another cloud layer.
Shackles	Terms found in the SOI that identified locations and were transmitted in code.
Short	Near the end of tour of duty, usually less than sixty days.
Short Final	Most critical part of approach to landing zone—the last 200 to 400 meters. Important factors: enemy condition, weight of aircraft (including fuel and cargo), wind velocity and direction, and size of LZ.
Skids	12 foot-long, strong, tubular landing support structure.
Skid Toe	Small flat step area located at top front of both skids.
Sky Raider	See "A-1."
Smoke, Smoke Grenade	Came in variety of colors used to signal others or mark positions and determine wind direction. Red used to mark enemy location.

SOI	Signal Operation Instructions. Top-secret code booklet issued only to aircraft commanders that contained call signs and radio frequencies.
SOP	Standard Operating Procedure.
Spotter Round	Artillery shell producing a dense cloud of white smoke upon impact, used to mark target or assist in adjusting fire.
Stage Field	A landing field in an outlying area. During training, pilots depart from the main helicopter base and fly to various training heliports where they practice and refuel. A stage field will normally have two parallel runways to practice autorotations.
Strack	Straight and squared away, a term used to describe or designate the ideal in military dress demeanor and bearing.
Strap Hangers	Slang for non-flying personnel, passengers.
Tactical	Military operation that is smaller and closer to base or headquarters, carried out in support of a larger operation.
Tet	Lunar New Year.
TH-55	Helicopter specifically used for training.
Tracer	Ammunition containing a chemical composition to mark the flight of projectiles (bullets) by a trail of fire.
Trail Formation	A flight formation in which one helicopter trails behind the other.
Troung Wi	Vietnamese First Lieutenant.
Typhoon	An Asian hurricane.
UHF	Ultra High Frequency military control towers and company-level communication. To "come up uniform" meant to dial in a predesignated UHF frequency.
Uniform	See "UHF."
V Formation	Flight formation that when viewed from below looks like the letter V.
VC	Viet Cong, the enemy.
VFR	Visual Flight Rules. Weather generally clear.

VHF	Very High Frequency. Mainly used for air-to-air communication, sometimes called just "Victor" for phonetic alphabet.
Victor	See "VHF."
Victor Zulu	Call sign for Australian officers during a combat operation.
VIP	Person of importance and influence commanding special treatment.
W1	Lowest rank Warrant Officer.
W2	Grade above 1, longer in service.
WD-1	Light, black, tactical telephone communication wire. Hand-carried spools held 1,300 to 5,000 feet each.
WIA	Wounded in Action.
Willy Pete	White, phosphorus artillery round or marking round.
WO	Warrant Officer. This rank has four grades, 1 through 4, junior to senior.
WOC	Warrant Officer Candidate, a flight school rank.
XO	Executive officer, second in command.
Zippo Lighter	Small, pocket-sized cigarette lighter, reusable and refillable, with metal case and hinged lid.

Phonetic Alphabet

A–Alpha
B–Bravo
C–Charlie
D–Delta
E–Echo
F–Foxtrot
G–Golf
H–Hotel
I–India

J–Juliet
K–Kilo
L–Lima
M–Mike
N–November
O–Oscar
P–Papa
Q–Quebec
R–Romeo

S–Sierra
T–Tango
U–Uniform
V–Victor
W–Whiskey
X–X-ray
Y–Yankee
Z–Zulu

Appendix

Excerpts From the MAY 69 Huey Technical Manual

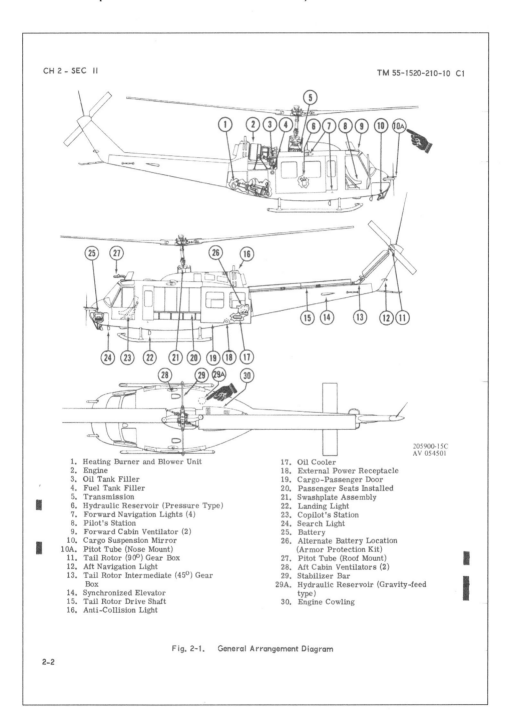

1. Heating Burner and Blower Unit
2. Engine
3. Oil Tank Filler
4. Fuel Tank Filler
5. Transmission
6. Hydraulic Reservoir (Pressure Type)
7. Forward Navigation Lights (4)
8. Pilot's Station
9. Forward Cabin Ventilator (2)
10. Cargo Suspension Mirror
10A. Pitot Tube (Nose Mount)
11. Tail Rotor (90°) Gear Box
12. Aft Navigation Light
13. Tail Rotor Intermediate (45°) Gear Box
14. Synchronized Elevator
15. Tail Rotor Drive Shaft
16. Anti-Collision Light

17. Oil Cooler
18. External Power Receptacle
19. Cargo-Passenger Door
20. Passenger Seats Installed
21. Swashplate Assembly
22. Landing Light
23. Copilot's Station
24. Search Light
25. Battery
26. Alternate Battery Location (Armor Protection Kit)
27. Pitot Tube (Roof Mount)
28. Aft Cabin Ventilators (2)
29. Stabilizer Bar
29A. Hydraulic Reservoir (Gravity-feed type)
30. Engine Cowling

205900-15C
AV 054501

Fig. 2-1.   General Arrangement Diagram

2-2

237

BLACK CAT 2-1

Excerpts From the MAY 69 Huey Technical Manual

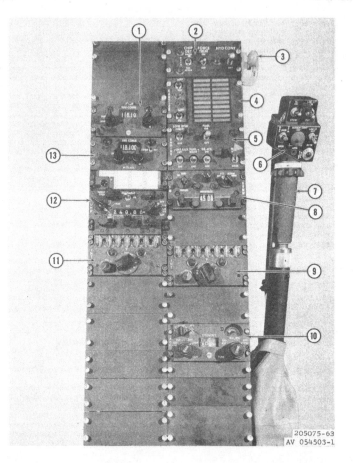

1. Navigation Control Panel C-6873/ARN-82
2. Hydraulic Control Panel
3. Heating Air Directing Lever
4. Caution Panel
5. Engine Control Panel
6. Switch Box - Collective Pitch Control Lever (Ref)
7. Collective Pitch Control Lever (Ref)
8. FM Control Panel C-3835/ARC-54
9. Signal Distribution Panel C-1611A/AIC
10. Direction Finder Control Panel - C6899/ARN-83
11. Signal Distribution Panel C-1611A/AIC
12. UHF Control Panel C-6287/ARC-51BX
13. VHF Control Panel C-7197/ARC-134

Figure 2-3. Pedestal panel installation - typical (Sheet 1 of 2)

Appendix

Excerpts From the MAY 69 Huey Technical Manual

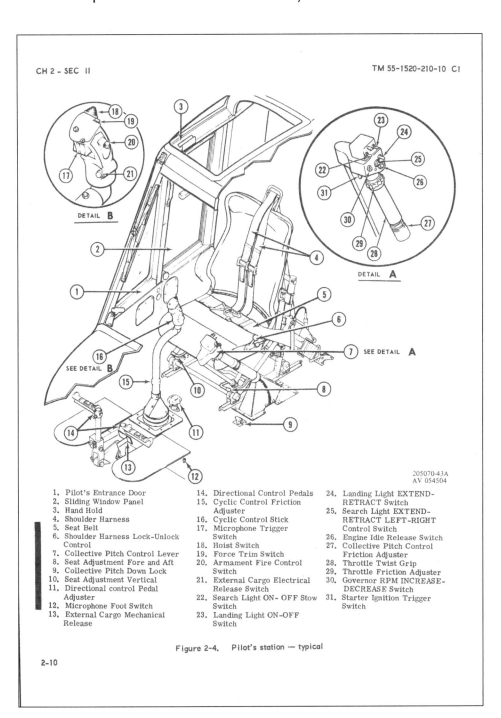

205070-43A
AV 054504

1. Pilot's Entrance Door
2. Sliding Window Panel
3. Hand Hold
4. Shoulder Harness
5. Seat Belt
6. Shoulder Harness Lock-Unlock Control
7. Collective Pitch Control Lever
8. Seat Adjustment Fore and Aft
9. Collective Pitch Down Lock
10. Seat Adjustment Vertical
11. Directional control Pedal Adjuster
12. Microphone Foot Switch
13. External Cargo Mechanical Release

14. Directional Control Pedals
15. Cyclic Control Friction Adjuster
16. Cyclic Control Stick
17. Microphone Trigger Switch
18. Hoist Switch
19. Force Trim Switch
20. Armament Fire Control Switch
21. External Cargo Electrical Release Switch
22. Search Light ON- OFF Stow Switch
23. Landing Light ON-OFF Switch

24. Landing Light EXTEND- RETRACT Switch
25. Search Light EXTEND- RETRACT LEFT-RIGHT Control Switch
26. Engine Idle Release Switch
27. Collective Pitch Control Friction Adjuster
28. Throttle Twist Grip
29. Throttle Friction Adjuster
30. Governor RPM INCREASE- DECREASE Switch
31. Starter Ignition Trigger Switch

Figure 2-4. Pilot's station — typical

2-10

239

Excerpts From the MAY 69 Huey Technical Manual

TM 55-1520-210-10 C1

CH 2 - SEC II

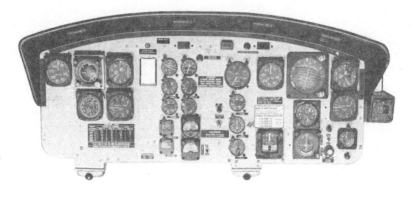

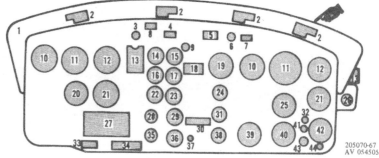

205070-67
AV 054505

1. Glare Shield	17. Engine Oil Temperature
2. Secondary Lights	Indicator
3. Engine Air Filter Light	18. Cargo Caution Decal
4. Master Caution	19. Dual Tachometer
5. RPM Warning Light	20. Radio Compass Indicator
6. Fire Detector Test Switch	21. Vertical Velocity Indicator
7. Fire Warning Indicator Light	22. Transmission Oil Pressure
8. Radio Call Designator	Indicator
9. Fuel Gage Test Switch	23. Transmission Oil Tempera-
10. Airspeed Indicator	ture Indicator
11. Attitude Indicator	24. Torquemeter Indicator
12. Altimeter Indicator	25. Radio Compass Indicator
13. Compass Correction Card	26. Standby Compass
Holder	27. Operating Limits Decal
14. Fuel Pressure Indicator	28. Main Generator Loadmeter
15. Fuel Quantity Indicator	29. DC Voltmeter
16. Engine Oil Pressure Indicator	30. Engine Caution Decal

31. Gas Producer Tachometer
Indicator
32. Marker Beacon Light
33. Engine Installation Decal
34. Transmitter Selector Decal
35. Standby Generator Loadmeter
36. AC Voltmeter
37. Compass Slaving Switch
38. Exhaust Gas Temperature
Indicator
39. Turn and Slip Indicator
40. Omni Indicator
41. Marker Beacon Sensing Switch
42. Clock
43. Marker Beacon Volume Control
44. Cargo Release Armed Light

Figure 2-5.   Instrument panel — typical

2-11

–About the Author–

From July 1967 to July 1968, Bob Ford flew over one thousand missions in Vietnam. After the first six weeks, he became an aircraft commander and took over the command of a helicopter detachment at Hue, forty miles from the DMZ—the farthest northern helicopter unit in Vietnam. His tour included the beginning of the siege of Khe Sahn and the Tet Offensive in February 1968 when he and his men manned the perimeter for a three-day and three-night ground attack.

Ford made his commitment to flying helicopters when he was still in college at the University of Oklahoma. He completed ROTC training and received a commission in the US Army in 1966. He volunteered for army helicopter flight school and within one year was flying combat in Vietnam. When he completed his tour in Vietnam, he became an instructor pilot at Fort Wolters, Texas. Following his discharge in 1969, he moved to Okeene, Oklahoma, to head the Okeene division of the family flour milling business, which he still actively manages.

(Mặt trận gửi binh sĩ Mỹ) 14 Dec '67

TO G.I.'S in Quảng-trị, Thừa-thiên, Huế!

The Vietnamese people are fighting against the aggressive, unjust Johnson's war for independence and freedom. The Vietnamese people and their strong armed forces have inflicted upon the one million odd Yanks and their lackeys heavy losses.

Hundred thousands Yanks died in Vietnam. The highway 9 and Quảng-trị, Thừa-thiên are the graveyard of the U.S. troops and the mercenaries from U.S. satellites.

G.I's! Don't be stupid enough to sacrifice yourself uselessly for the selfish and dirty interests of Johnson. Your happiness is not to be found in Vietnam, but in your sweet home in the U.S.A.

G.I'S!

—Refuse to carry out criminal orders! Say NO to raiding burning destroying killing!

—Refuse battle! Demand to be sent home!

—When attacked, let be captured, and you will be granted leniency and treated with humanity.

The Tri-Thiên-Huế's L.A.F. ...

I spotted this leaflet blowing around when we landed in an LZ and asked the crew chief to retrieve it. We all got a laugh when I read it over the intercom.

–Photos–

Prologue

Sandy Boeckman's third grade class

The original NOV 67 Polaroid of the Black Cats: standing, Lieutenant Bob Ford, W-2 Dwight Dedrick, W-1 Mark Skulborstad, and W-2 Tom Pullen; seated, W-1 John Aye, W-2 Al Toews, W-2 Jerry McKinsey, and W-1 Dick Messer

Chapter 1

Major Chuck Ward

The armored seats in our Hueys stopped any small arms fire; our vests protected us from front fire.

Flying right seat

At Marble Mountain; eleven more months in Vietnam

After combat assault; two weeks in country; W2 Harold Hebert is on the left, I'm in the middle, and SP4 Baker is on the right.

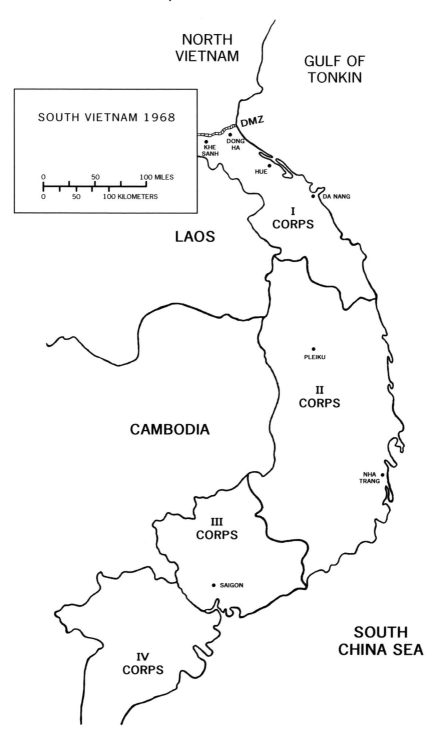

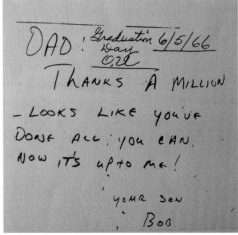

Chapter 2

A note I wrote to my dad that he dated on my college graduation day.

Fort Wolters, front gate, 1966. Left: OH-23, Right: TH-55

This is one of three "mug shots" taken at the beginning of flight school for identification in case of a crash.

With my solo aircraft

My solo dunk in the ditch—
even my yellow hat got soaked.

With the Bell H-13

Hughes TH-55

Celebrating my wings with Diane,
June 30, 1967

Saying good-bye at Will
Rogers World Airport

FROM THE DESK OF ---

Leslie A. Ford   Copy

7/22/67

Dear Bob —

This is from Bill & me for your Birthday present.

You are now leaving to serve your Country in a foreign land for a year. You will meet & make new friends — you also will be among some rough & hostile people.

In all you do, remember your training to be a gentleman & be fair. Take care of yourself.

Your lovely wife, Diane, & your entire family extend love & prayers for your safe return,

Your Dad.

Note from my dad

Chapter 3

Alley Cat attack gunship with heavy armament: revetment shows impact of mortar attack.

Chapter 4

Lennis Lee, Black Cat 2-2

Chapter 5

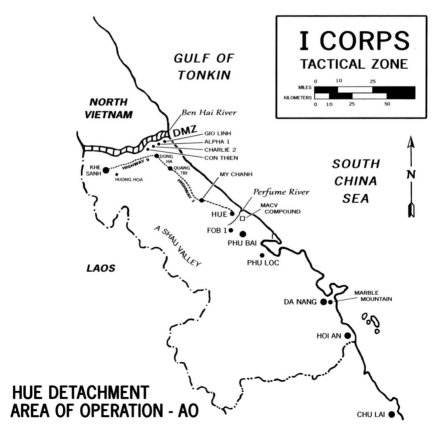

HUE DETACHMENT
AREA OF OPERATION - AO

Crashed Caribou at La Vang

Flying low level down Highway 1

Flying low level over rice paddies

```
                    DEPARTMENT OF THE ARMY
                282ND ASSAULT HELICOPTER COMPANY
               212TH COMBAT SUPPORT AVIATION BATTALION
                    APO San Francisco  96337

UNIT ORDERS                                    13 September 1967
NUMBER   84

        1.  TC 350.  Fol indiv this sta APPOINTED.

ZELTNER, RICHARD L. 098351 CPT CE 282nd Aslt Hel Co APO 96337
FORD, ROBERT L. 05422346 1LT TC 282nd Aslt Hel Co APO 96337
COLBURN, EDWARD B. W3155835 WO1 AVN 282nd Aslt Hel Co APO 96337
   Apt to:  Aircraft Commander in UH-1D
   Eff date:  13 Sep 67
   Pd:  While assigned to the 282nd Avn Co unless sooner  recinded
   Auth:  AR 95-4, dtd 16 Jun 65, w/changes
   Sp instr:  An aircraft  commander is responsible for matters pertaining
              to successful mission accomplishment.




                                        Charles E Ward Jr.
                                        CHARLES E. WARD JR.
                                        Major, Infantry
                                        Commanding

DISTRIBUTION:
   9- Personnel Section
   9- S-1
   9- 282nd Aslt Hel Co, Opns
   2- Indiv conc
   1- Order file
```

My AC orders

Landing south at Hue Airfield

Perfume River Bridge

Entering the MACV Compound

American flag flying over the
MACV Compound

Hue MACV Compound

The Black Cats Hue detachment, NOV 67: standing, Lieutenant Bob Ford, W-2 Dwight Dedrick, W-1 Mark Skulborstad, and W-2 Tom Pullen; seated, W-1 John Aye, W-2 Al Toews, W-2 Jerry McKinsey, and W-1 Dick Messer

Chapter 6

Tom Pullen is holding his "bulldog"—a modified M2 carbine.
I am holding in both arms my issued M16. Revetments in background
are made from fifty-five-gallon Agent Orange barrels.

Flying over Da Nang Bay

F-4 Phantom

Tom Pullen, OCT 67—became Black Cat 2-7

Chapter 7

Dong Ha POL

One minute after refueling
Dong Ha took several direct hits.

Crew Chief Joe Sumner

Chapter 8

In the left seat

Chapter 8 (continued)

NVA officers taken
prisoner; the first I'd seen
tagged and blindfolded

Wounded prisoners of war

Chapter 9

Zippo Lighter

Flying VFR on top

Resupply of troops west of
Hue near A Shau Valley—
landed in bomb crater

Flying feet wet

The *Repose*

Chapter 10

B-52 strike

Pham Thi Bon

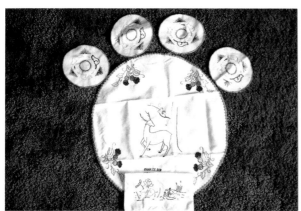

Pham Thi Bon's gift

Chapter 11

Highway 9

DMZ outpost Alpha 1

DMZ outpost Charlie 1

Colonel Peter Kelley,
General Lam, Vietnamese
premier Nguyen Cao Ky,
and General Truong

Main Street in Hue along the Perfume
River where we dropped
the Christmas gum to the kids

B-29

Another view of Main Street in Hue

Bud Atanian, outstanding crew
chief—they all were

"Christmas" smoke grenades over
the MACV Compound

Bob Hope and Raquel Welch

The picture of Diane I
kept inside my SOI

Perimeter defenses at Huong Hoa

Jerry McKinsey,
MAR 67—new
in country

Jerry McKinsey, holding blood chit, NOV 67:
we both stopped for chow at the same LZ.

My bunker—
entrance on right

Desi and me

This photographer showed up the
second or third day of the battle.
She is standing on a jeep near the
front gate taking pictures.

Marines manning the .50-caliber
that broke through to the
MACV Compound

261

Chapter 15 (continued)

James Payne, McColon, Lowell "Dee" Truscott, and Bob Brown in the
Hue Compound before evacuation to Da Nang, 03 FEB 68

Chapter 16

One of our Huey D models after a rocket attack at Marble Mountain during Tet

Deuce and a half truck bringing marine WIA: ammunition
and supplies we brought in are stacked by the truck.

Outpost we resupplied
southwest of the
Citadel. Australian
Terry Egan, on the right
in the landing zone,
sent this picture to me.
He wrote on the back:
"You were here."

Bart Colburn on his
wedding day, JUN 68

Chapter 17

Diane ready to go out
to see Don Ho

Enjoying my time away
from the war

Seeing the sights in Hawaii

With the '67 Camaro
in front of the Hilton
Hawaiian Village

Tripler Army Medical Center

Chapter 18

The Citadel took a pounding. It was good to see the South Vietnamese flying where the VC flag had flown for ten days during Tet.

What was left of Hue Airfield after Tet

Our Huey after Tet

Remnants of one of our two aircraft

Chapter 18 (continued)

Hue Airfield, MAR 68:
preparing for a
combat assault

Southeast corner of the MACV Compound after Tet; Warrants' bunker
where Dedrick was killed in action. My bunker is to the immediate right of
theirs. Trees in foreground where sniper was shot

USS *Newport News*

Chapter 19

Door gunner James Payne in background; ARVN soldiers in foreground

Resupplying a mountaintop outpost during monsoons—as hard to find it as to land there

Chapter 20

These tank antennas were tempting targets.

Chapter 21

Empty casing picked up

Live round found in AK-47

Chapter 23

Over the A Shau Valley
en route to Laos

Laos en route second time
to pick up the Nung

Last soldier out

Our Cobra escorts
back at FOB-1

Chapter 24

Jim Burnett

Coordinating another
northern mission with
Al Toews

Wearing my captain's
bars and the jungle
fatigues given to
me by the First
Cavalry captain

Last in line at Da Nang Airfield, loading onto the C-130
headed to Cam Ranh Bay and then home

I made it back; brother Bill made this sign for me at my home in Shawnee.

With Amy

Beach Army Hospital

My brother, Bill, introduced me at the Huey dedication ceremony and is sitting just to my left. Crew Chief Jerry Staggs is far right.

Oklahoma Veterans Park in Shawnee

Epilogue (continued)

Finishing 1.5-mile open water course, state championship triathlon, Edmond, Oklahoma

Finishing the bike course, Wichita Falls, Texas

Competing in Ironman Canada, Penticton, British Columbia; about mile eight of the marathon

With my grandkids— Cate Bradley, Emma Bradley, Taylor Lewis, Tess Bradley, and Nathan Lewis—in front of Ford Family Log Cabin outside Shawnee, Oklahoma

Veterans Day 2012 with my daughter Allison and granddaughter Taylor

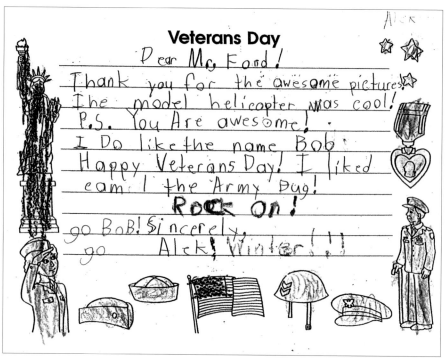

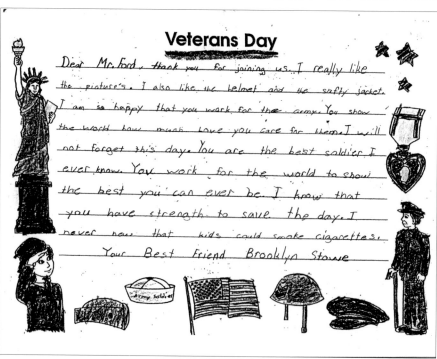

Typical letters from Okeene third grade boys and girls

Children of Vietnam

I always told my own children that we never want to fight a war in our own country because of the toll it takes on the kids. Their lives were horribly impacted by the war, but being so young, they were always ready to smile and ask us for food from our C-rations. All of the following pictures were taken at friendly LZs while we were shut down for chow.

Kids did not wear pants until they were toilet trained.

This was the cleanest kid I ever saw in Vietnam.

These kids with South Vietnamese flags were as neat and clean as possible.

Children of Vietnam (continued)

I rarely saw a child wearing shoes. This picture was taken during monsoon season near Cam Lo. A soggy Highway 9 is in the background.

I was told no American could ride a water buffalo. I accepted the challenge. Specialist 4 Jakushev made sure the kid holding the rope that went through the buffalo's nose did not yank it.

Jakushev with the usual gathering: when they saw our Black Cat, the kids came running. They knew we would treat them well.

Christmas Day 1967 at an orphanage east of Phu Tu

Children of Vietnam (continued)

A sunny day—four are standing
in the shadow of our rotor blade.

We looked forward to
their playful antics.

All the kids were
our friends.

This photo more than any other made an impression on the third graders
in Okeene. The young boy, about six, at Phu Loc LZ, is holding a four-
pack of cigarettes that came in every C-ration meal. After I handed a
cigarette to him from the cockpit, I reached down and lit it and said,
"Salute, troung wi," and snapped this near-perfect picture.

Refueling at Hue between missions. Nov 67